"Jonathan Brooks ('Pastah J') is one of the most authentic, credible, and prophetic voices in the church today. *Church Forsaken* is a holy wake-up call for every Christian to not overlook the beauty in the brokenness around us. This book will have you looking for the glory of God in every place and person, including yourself."

Shawn Casselberry, executive director of Mission Year, coauthor of *Soul Force: Seven Pivots Toward Courage, Community, and Change*

"*Church Forsaken* brilliantly demonstrates that we love God by loving our neighbor, and one of the primary ways we love our neighbor is by loving our neighborhood. This book is a bold dare to all followers of Jesus to (re) discover the scale of God's good news by becoming faithfully present within our parishes, not just as individuals, but as the body of Christ."

Dwight J. Friesen, associate professor of practical theology at the Seattle School of Theology & Psychology, author of *Thy Kingdom Connected*

"Jonathan Brooks is a leader of our time whose commitment to local community, the church, and people gives us an example of pastoral presence that is quite inspiring. Jonathan's commitment to place goes unmatched. The choice to return to a neighborhood that many escape from radiates hope. The stories display the power of presence from unexpected places and push us to believe."

Leroy Barber, cofounder of The Voices Project, director of innovation at the United Methodist Church Greater Northwest

"Theology of place is one of the most critical foundations of community transformation. Pastor Jonathan Brooks outlines a biblical and practical approach to understanding the importance of location in the life of a church and Christian communities. The stories told, mistakes made, and victories won in this book are authentic and relevant. I have longed for a book with this level of integrity and wisdom on the topic of the church intentionally living *in* and *with* a community. No fronting or faking here."

Sandra Maria Van Opstal, pastor, activist, author of *The Next Worship*

"I don't know a more faithful, committed, and compassionate person when it comes to caring for one's neighborhood and truly *living* the gospel of Jesus Christ. Jonathan is for the people—for the hearts and souls that make up a community. He calls all of us good church folk to fall in love with our neighborhoods and join in with the work of renewal that God is up to in communities. *Church Forsaken* is a call to remember who we are for and what's at stake when we forget each other."

Rozella Haydée White, owner of Restoring Hearts to Wholeness LLC

"Jonathan Brooks beautifully weaves the lessons he's learned on his journey as a pastor in Chicago's Englewood neighborhood with the instructions the Israelites are given while in exile in Babylon (Jeremiah 29). The questions he raises about *where* and *with whom* get to the heart of the vision he sees for Christians and the local church."

Mackenzi Huyser, executive director of Chicago Semester, professor of social work at Trinity Christian College

"In this book you will find the future of the church—faithfully present, contagiously hopeful, and unflinchingly honest. Jonathan Brooks has written a must-read book that draws from his very particular life and neighborhood, but has universal lessons that are critical for all of us. Stop what you are doing and read this book—it's that important."

Tim Soerens, coauthor of *The New Parish,* cofounder of the Inhabit Conference

"Jonathan Brooks is a phenomenal pastor. In *Church Forsaken,* he weaves his story of deep pastoring experience with very practical and theological truths through his church and community ministry. Jonathan's personal story is powerful and has helped me be a better pastor. I loved reading this book and so will you."

Wayne Gordon, founding pastor of Lawndale Community Church, chairman of CCDA

"Working closely with Pastah J has really helped me shift my perspective about the black church. Pastah J showed me and others in our association R.A.G.E. that there are faith-based leaders who understand and embrace their role as a valuable asset in our communities. He is thoughtful and sensitive to the issues in our neighborhood and continues to work collectively with not only the members of his church but with the entire Greater Englewood community."

Asiaha Butler, cofounder and president, Resident Association of Greater Englewood (R.A.G.E.)

"Jonathan Brooks's voice and leadership are rooted in Scripture and grounded in his community. In *Church Forsaken,* the story of Jonathan's Englewood community in Chicago unfolds alongside the story of Jeremiah. Jonathan explores the connections between calling and community, activism and service, and the power in partnership. Let the words here convict you, challenge you, and call you home."

Amena Brown, spoken-word poet, author of *How to Fix a Broken Record*

"Nobody—and I mean *nobody*—tells it like Jonathan Brooks! Our neighborhoods are not God forsaken—they are *church* forsaken. Get your people together and go deep into these chapters. It's time to start praying and plotting the return of the local church. *Church Forsaken* is the wake-up call we have needed. But beware—the ringtone is jacked into hip-hop beats, street preaching, and some of the most binge-worthy front porch storytelling you can find. I'm giving it to everyone."

Paul Sparks, cofounding director of the Parish Collective, coauthor of *The New Parish*

"Pastor Jonathan Brooks and Canaan Community Church are a true model of what it means to be a fully engaged church in a vulnerable community that needs it the most. As a lifelong West Englewood resident and current state legislator, I love the way *Church Forsaken* calls on faith-based communities to boldly and unapologetically take on their proper role. When more churches take on the role that Pastah J explains in his book, we will see the changes we truly want to see finally come to fruition in our communities both in the city of Chicago and throughout the state of Illinois."

Sonya Harper, representative from Illinois, 6th District

"In *Church Forsaken*, pastor Jonathan Brooks courageously offers us an inspired and compelling vision of a relevant church that radically engages urban landscapes and contexts everywhere the gospel's transformative power is needed. As a thoughtful, servant leader of a local church serving a neighborhood where violence and poverty can steal the innocence of children and tear at the fabric of families—Pastah J's compelling vision of a relevant church continues in the best prophetic traditions of Dr. Martin Luther King Jr. and Dietrich Bonhoeffer."

Vance T. Henry, chief of Faith-Based Partnerships and Initiatives, city of Chicago, Office of the Mayor

"The Chicago Children's Choir was founded at the height of the civil rights movement by a pastor who understood that Christ's concept of the church was not intended to be bound by four walls but to be out thriving and nurturing our communities. *Church Forsaken* is a testimony to this belief and that the work of Christ is a work of service—starting with those closest to you. Pastor Brooks's story challenges us all to measure love in our actions—not words—and inspires the desire to do so! I recommend anyone involved in community and urban development, regardless of religious affiliation, read this book!"

Josephine Lee, president and artistic director, Chicago Children's Choir

"I have known Pastor Jonathan Brooks for over two decades and I have been humbled to serve alongside him and observe his never-wavering tenacity to live, function, and totally embody his prophetic voice for this generation. Pastah J is not writing out of some studied theory but truly personifies the theology of place outlined in *Church Forsaken*. If half the churches in the United States took to heart the words from this book, we would truly see revival and true transformation."

Phil Jackson, pastor of The House, founder and executive director of The Firehouse Community Arts Center

"With the help of Jay-Z, Jeremiah, and Chance the Rapper, my brother Jonathan Brooks offers a prophetic and pragmatic vision that has us doing backflips. Pastah J reminds us that redemption requires putting down roots, that love requires listening, that loving our neighbor requires serving our neighborhoods, and that the gospel is not just interested in your soul but creation as a whole."

Jarrod McKenna, pastor, peace award–winning social change educator, host of InVerse and Perisson

"Many pastors invest a lot of marketing dollars to rebrand the church. What I appreciate about Jonathan Brooks is that he's invested time and presence to rebrand the church within his local community. *Church Forsaken* is rich in a wisdom that only comes out of practicing what he preaches. Whether you live in a favored or forgotten neighborhood, I highly recommend this book if you want to be a local church."

David M. Bailey, executive director of Arrabon, founder of Urban Doxology

"Jonathan Brooks issues a clarion call to his readers by inviting us to release the idol of comfort in exchange for the ministry of practicing presence. The way of Jesus is the way of unconditional and sacrificial love; Pastah J takes us by the hand and shows us how our welfare is bound up in the welfare of our neighbors, neighborhood, and city."

Ekemini Uwan, public theologian, cohost of Truth's Table podcast

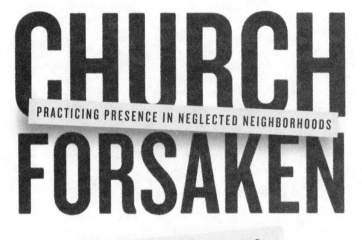

CHURCH FORSAKEN

PRACTICING PRESENCE IN NEGLECTED NEIGHBORHOODS

JONATHAN BROOKS

FOREWORD BY SHO BARAKA

IVP Books

An imprint of InterVarsity Press
Downers Grove, Illinois

InterVarsity Press
P.O. Box 1400, Downers Grove, IL 60515-1426
ivpress.com
email@ivpress.com

InterVarsity Press® is the book-publishing division of InterVarsity Christian Fellowship/USA®, a movement of students and faculty active on campus at hundreds of universities, colleges, and schools of nursing in the United States of America, and a member movement of the International Fellowship of Evangelical Students. For information about local and regional activities, visit intervarsity.org.

Scripture quotations, unless otherwise noted, are from the New Revised Standard Version of the Bible, copyright 1989 by the Division of Christian Education of the National Council of the Churches of Christ in the USA. Used by permission. All rights reserved.

While any stories in this book are true, some names and identifying information may have been changed to protect the privacy of individuals.

Cover design: David Fassett
Interior design: Daniel van Loon
Images: church doors: © catnap72 / E+ / Getty Images
    closed sign: © titaniumdoughnut / E+ / Getty Images
    grunge design elements: © ulimi / Digital Vision Vectors / Getty Images
    red wall with secured door: © JM_Image_Factory / Istock / Getty Images Plus
    spray paint grunge: © Thoth_Adan / Digital Vision Vectors / Getty Images

ISBN 978-0-8308-4555-2 (print)
ISBN 978-0-8308-7371-5 (digital)

Printed in the United States of America ♾

InterVarsity Press is committed to ecological stewardship and to the conservation of natural resources in all our operations. This book was printed using sustainably sourced paper.

Library of Congress Cataloging-in-Publication Data
Names: Brooks, Jonathan, 1979- author.
Title: Church forsaken : practicing presence in neglected neighborhoods / Jonathan Brooks.
Description: Downers Grove : InterVarsity Press, 2018. | Includes bibliographical references.
Identifiers: LCCN 2018028316 (print) | LCCN 2018035838 (ebook) | ISBN 9780830873715 (eBook) | ISBN 9780830845552 (pbk. : alk. paper)
Subjects: LCSH: Communities—Religious aspects—Christianity. | Neighborhoods. | Church work with the poor.
Classification: LCC BV625 (ebook) | LCC BV625 .B76 2018 (print) | DDC 250—dc23
LC record available at https://lccn.loc.gov/2018028316

P 25 24 23 22 21 20 19 18 17 16 15 14 13 12 11 10 9 8 7 6 5 4 3 2 1

Y 37 36 35 34 33 32 31 30 29 28 27 26 25 24 23 22 21 20 19 18

Dedicated to the memory of Martinez Newman.

I promise to always take care of your ladies.

Gone too soon but never forgotten.

Thus says the LORD of hosts, the God of Israel, to all the exiles whom I have sent into exile from Jerusalem to Babylon: Build houses and live in them; plant gardens and eat what they produce. Take wives and have sons and daughters; take wives for your sons, and give your daughters in marriage, that they may bear sons and daughters; multiply there, and do not decrease. But seek the welfare of the city where I have sent you into exile, and pray to the LORD on its behalf, for in its welfare you will find your welfare. For thus says the LORD of hosts, the God of Israel: Do not let the prophets and the diviners who are among you deceive you, and do not listen to the dreams that they dream, for it is a lie that they are prophesying to you in my name; I did not send them, says the LORD.

For thus says the LORD: Only when Babylon's seventy years are completed will I visit you, and I will fulfill to you my promise and bring you back to this place. For surely I know the plans I have for you, says the LORD, plans for your welfare and not for harm, to give you a future with hope.

JEREMIAH 29:4-11

CONTENTS

SHO BARAKA

Anything will give up its secrets if you love it enough." This pithy statement came from the revolutionary botanist George Washington Carver. Some say he single-handedly saved southern agriculture from soil depletion with his plant-based discoveries. Droves would travel across time zones to hear Carver's brilliance. Science had never spawned such an agrarian innovator.

Just as notable as his contributions was his posture of humility. This is because Carver knew the secrets to his success were not his. The secrets of flourishing were revealed in his compassionate transactions with God's creation. Carver parried offers of promising wealth to continue his revolutionary practices at a demure Tuskegee Institute. The masses were perplexed and unsatisfied with his answers, but in his unassuming way Carver revealed, "Not only have I found that when I talk to the little flower or little peanut it will give up its secrets, but I have found that when I silently commune with people they give up their secrets also."[1]

At this same modest institution I met Jonathan Brooks, or John as I came to call him. Our friendship blossomed at Tuskegee

University on the same Alabama clay that bloomed many great progenies before us. We were kindred in our affinity for hip-hop culture and quasi-philosophical discourses that were above our acumen and course syllabus. I must admit he was a much more promising student than me. To my bewilderment, he would often lose weekends in the Wilcox buildings laboring over architecture projects with dozens of others in the *intelligentsia*. So it was a bit of a shock to learn years later that my friend John, an extremely talented architect, had become a pastor.

There was something within John Brooks that didn't come from the Robert Taylor School of Architecture. In college his presence was ubiquitous and comforting. He was a magnet that many of us didn't know we needed. He was a unifier without the flattery. If anyone could maintain relationships with old friends or acquaintances, it was John. Like George W. Carver, John could also speak to flowers. Only his flowers were a different variety. I believe he discovered that he could architect *flourishing* in a way that no firm could construct.

Like many black folks that come from neglected communities, John was told that success was achieved by how far you could get from that community and its snares. But these same communities also made him who he is today. The academic and religious institutions cannot claim sole responsibility in making Jonathan Brooks. He is also a product of tenacious parenting, persistent ingenuity, hip-hop culture, and the vibrant social settings of the south side of Chicago.

It didn't take long for these elements to finesse their way into his pulpit. He used hip-hop as a medium to engage and make complex issues simple. He soon transformed from Jonathan Brooks to Pastah J. His ingenuity innovated in ways beyond his resources. He ultimately found himself back in the community he was told to escape.

John has learned that if he quietly communes with people, he will learn their secrets. He doesn't have all the answers, so he speaks to the flowers in his community. When his church created a scholarship fund, it was because he spoke to the flowers. When his church partnered with community entrepreneurs to create the only coworking gathering space and cafe in miles, it was because he spoke to the flowers. When his church developed a cooperative food program, it was because he spoke to the flowers.

He is a modest man who pastors a modest church, practicing humility and presence in a way that is simple. With all the good his church is doing, he has little desire to raise his public profile. He rightly displays how the church is the empirical evidence of God's blessing to a community.

I exhort the reader to be challenged by the anecdotes of Jonathan Brooks's theology of place without feeling the compulsion to replicate them. The principles transcend the methods. You can travel across time zones to investigate the secrets of his fruitful labor, but I caution you to not be disconcerted by simple answers. He simply listens to the flowers in the garden that God has placed him in.

PRACTICE ONE

RESIDE WHERE YOU DON'T WANT TO BE

THE CHURCH-FORSAKEN POSITION

Thus says the LORD of hosts, the God of
Israel, to all the exiles whom I have sent
into exile from Jerusalem to Babylon.

JEREMIAH 29:4

FROM THE MIND OF AN EXILE

A s I sat on my enclosed porch reading a book and enjoying the cool breeze flowing through the windows, instantly my tranquil July evening was interrupted with the sound of gunfire. I quickly jumped up to run into the house, but as I reached for the door a group of young men came running down my alley. I watched the direction they ran in case I needed to provide some information for the police. After about ten minutes I heard the sirens of the police and ambulance. Like most of my other neighbors, once it seemed to be safe I made my way to the alley to see if everyone was okay. Unfortunately, everyone was not alright. A young man named L'Terrick had been killed by gunshot in the alley right behind my house. Along with the pain, fear, and frustration of dealing with my hurting neighbors, many of whom are connected to our church, the typical questions arose from my friends and family who live outside of our neighborhood and care about my family: Why don't you move? Why don't you go somewhere else? You don't have to live there. Why are you there? In these intense moments it is often difficult to think of proper responses to these questions.

Chicago is known as a city of neighborhoods—rightfully so, as we have seventy-seven well-defined communities on the North, South, and West Sides. I reside in the West Englewood community on the South Side, which is notorious to some but beloved to others. Local residents often use the term "Greater Englewood" to describe our community since it is composed of two tight-knit neighborhoods that sit side by side: Englewood and West Englewood. When I speak of my community, I may use Greater Englewood, West Englewood, or Englewood interchangeably.

In the 1960s, advances in civil rights opened more areas of housing to blacks, and many moved to Englewood, West Englewood, and other South Side neighborhoods. By the turn of the century this influx of African Americans had been accompanied by "white flight" and disinvestment by the city. This resulted in the loss of jobs, poor housing conditions, and an increase in violence. During the subsequent decades the population of Englewood declined by nearly thirty thousand residents. This phenomenon was not only limited to individual families but entire institutions, and the local church was no exception. In his book *Shades of White Flight*, which discusses the Christian Reformed Church's flight from South Side neighborhoods, Mark T. Mulder states,

> Within these highly socially isolated religious communities there are such weak ties to the broader neighborhood that members are easily predisposed to mobility: when they felt their neighborhood threatened by the arrival of African Americans they did not take very long to pack up and reconstitute themselves in the suburbs.[1]

Although we've had quite a few violent episodes like this in our neighborhood, contrary to popular belief it is not an everyday occurrence. As a matter of fact, just like in any other neighborhood, it's a really big deal when a shooting happens, especially if it is fatal. Families are devastated and entire blocks are gripped with fear. It is personally traumatic and shakes the foundations of my family and my life and often makes me ask very difficult questions. In other words, contrary to what you may have heard about neighborhoods like West Englewood, it's not commonplace for lives to be snatched away violently, for things to feel as though they are falling apart, or for mothers to lose their children before they experience all that life has to offer.

Events like these often leave me grasping for answers to life's hard questions and many times have caused me to doubt God and struggle with my faith. How could a loving God allow such evil to happen in the world? However, as I meditated on this question this time, it felt as if God was asking me a similar question. How can such loving people, who live on these same blocks, allow such evil to happen? While I did not receive an answer to my question, it was becoming increasingly clear that I had no right to question God's intervention until I began to answer God's question about my own intervention. God was reminding me that the plan has always been for us to be involved in the redemption of the world, not to be spectators complaining on the sidelines.

THE PLACE YOU DON'T WANT TO BE

The passage in Jeremiah 29 that I unpack in this book is the impetus for the way I understand God's plan for humanity in the world. Jeremiah writes this letter to Israel because they have completely gone away from God's plan for their life. The expectation was for them to be a godly example and tangible expression of God's presence to the surrounding nations, but they had become insular and concerned only with themselves. The mark of a caring society is their love for the most marginalized people, and God repeatedly sent prophets to remind Israel of their social responsibility.

As a matter of fact, the letter is addressed to "all the exiles whom I have sent into exile" (Jeremiah 29:4). It says, "I have sent," because it is God who sent them to exile. They didn't make the decision.

They didn't get to choose. Initially exile is due to the poor choices of God's people. However, the following generation is born in exile even though they had nothing to do with the initial poor decisions. This feels familiar to many of the young people I work with and the families I counsel, and even myself at times. We too were born into chronically neglected neighborhoods and have all felt exiled in the communities where we were placed by God. Just like the exiles in our passage, the issues in these often-forgotten communities were not initiated by the actions of the current residents. Yet they still find themselves enduring similar suffering and often perpetuating the same poor decisions.

While this book is in no way meant to be an academic endeavor, I want to begin by sharing with you my working theological definition of *exile*. It is foundational for understanding my story and how this passage of Scripture has been used to reveal God's hand in my life. It is a simple definition that is based on a lifetime of experiential research. Simply put, I define *exile* as "the place you don't want to be."

A community resident once told me he believes that there are only two kinds of people who live in Englewood: those who have no other place to go, and those who have no other place they'd rather be. Ultimately, that makes for a bunch of exceptional people! When residents of a community feel trapped, they work extremely hard to find avenues that will help them create what they consider to be a better life. No one wants to feel stuck or as if they have no choices, but this is the reality for many in inner-city communities all over America. We know this simply by looking at the actions of those raised in these communities who are deemed successful by society's standards. Professional athletes know that the first thing you do once you make a lot of money is move away from your inner-city community. It is honorable to give back your time and resources, but it is considered foolish to remain there or move back once you are economically stable.

The 90s hip-hop artist Notorious B.I.G. says in his song "Things Done Changed,"

Because the streets is a short stop
Either you're slinging crack rock or you got a wicked
jump shot[2]

Basically, he's saying that people in his inner-city neighborhood didn't have many options when it came to their future choices. They either sold drugs or tried to make it as professional athletes. Either way, they were not going to be on the block for long: it was just a "short stop." This speaks to the bleakness of his surroundings as a youth. Just about anybody who has been deemed successful from neighborhoods like these has moved away. It is understood that to be successful means to move away. If you found yourself still living in your neighborhood or in a similar economic state as your childhood, even if it was lower middle class, you had failed. Honestly, I grew up believing the same things. Young people from communities like mine already reside in the place we don't want to be. It's not some strange place to which we are banished because of disobedience. Unlike Israel in Babylon, home is the last place on earth we want to be.

Of course, conversely, there are residents who have made the decision to remain or return to these communities for various reasons. These are the people who believe there is no other place they would rather live, and their reasons for returning or remaining are as diverse as they are. Take my friends Aja and Kelvin McLanahan, for instance, who moved back into a family home in Englewood because they are committed to living within their financial means and increasing them. They are currently debt free. Now they partner with community organizations and churches to teach others how to do the same.

Some have remained for decades because of vigor for the community and its residents and have been working to see the amazing people of the community achieve their dreams and aspirations. Mrs. Patricia Divine-Reed, a member of our church, has been working and living on the South Side of Chicago for decades and was the creator of the Boulevard Arts Center. This program reached thousands of youth on the South Side with the arts and was a beacon of hope in the Englewood community during the late 1980s and early 1990s. Some have moved into these neighborhoods because they have fallen in love with the history, camaraderie, and true sense of community. My friend Phil Sipka, an Englewood transplant, worked with a group of community residents to open the Kusanya Café, a resident-owned restaurant and gathering space. Just as in any other community, longtime residents who have remained in the neighborhood will often reminisce about the "good ole days" when things were supposedly so much better—though they know there have always been "challenges with changes," as James Stampley put it in his 1979 book chronicling Englewood's developmental journey.[3]

I understand both perspectives. I was once a young man who was itching to get as far away as possible from my neighborhood. I traveled to Tuskegee University in Alabama for college, with the hope of never returning to Chicago. If I did return, it would not be to the same economic situation or neighborhood. I studied architecture rather than art or music because I needed to be confident that I could move the economic class needle forward for my family. Where I ended up economically and geographically at the end of this journey was paramount to my understanding of success. Now, twenty years later, as an unplanned return resident, I love Englewood passionately and couldn't imagine living anywhere else. So what caused this drastic change? What brought about this 180-degree turn in a young man's mind about a place he had classified as exile?

After reflecting on my journey and the letter in Jeremiah 29, I began to change the way I looked at my "exilic" situation. I had been unconsciously asking questions like: Why did I have to be born in Englewood? Why couldn't I be born out in a quiet suburb? Why did I have to be born to a single mother struggling every day? God, what did I do to you?

God has been responding, sometimes rather vividly, saying, "Let me show you what you can learn from your seemingly unfortunate circumstances."

GOD FORSAKEN?

One question I am often asked is where these incomplete narratives about certain communities originate. Are they all incorrect since a disproportionate amount of violence and crime do happen there? I believe the origin of these narratives is deeper than statistics and reports. It is an underlying belief that the presence of God is absent there. In our Jeremiah passage it is a juxtaposition of two places, Israel and Babylon, that create the understandings. For the exiles, Israel is the place where God dwells, while Babylon represents a place where God is not present. This belief that Babylon was a God-forsaken place and the Babylonians a God-forsaken people was the main reason they did not want to be there. This is why Jeremiah has to write a letter reminding the exiles that there is no place they can go where the hand of God cannot reach them. If we were to get down to our underlying belief about certain communities, it would echo this sentiment. There are certain people and places that we believe God's presence has yet to reach. Not only do we believe God's presence has yet to reach them but sometimes even that God's presence has fled and abandoned them, which, in turn, gives us permission to do the same.

When weather permits, on Sunday mornings I like to walk from my house to the church. However, one September morning I decided to drive down Garfield Boulevard to take in the beautiful landscape of the midway and clear my mind. When I reached the Dan Ryan Expressway, which is about two miles east of my house, I saw a man selling newspapers (along with theologian Karl Barth, I believe preachers should hold the Bible in one hand and the newspaper in the other.) I thought it would be a great idea to purchase a paper and see what events had taken place that weekend, as I prepared to lead my congregation that morning. Once I reached the stoplight, I rolled down my window and motioned for him to come over so I could grab a paper.

"Sunday *Sun-Times,* please" I said politely.

"That'll be a buck fifty," he responded with a smile.

I reached into my cup holder, pulled out six quarters, and dropped them into his right hand. He began to pull one of the papers from the stack nestled carefully between his body and his left arm. As he grabbed the top newspaper from the stack he looked at it with disdain.

Then he shook his head and said to me, "It's a shame how they do people."

Not having seen the paper yet, I had no clue what he meant, but it did not take me long to understand his look of disdain or his penetrating words. On the front page of the *Chicago Sun-Times* Sunday paper, the largest and most widely read paper of the week, was a photo of a distraught woman with blood gushing from her mouth against a pitch-black background. Above the photo in bold red letters was the headline "A Good Day in Englewood." The caption read, "A bleeding woman yells at police during a domestic-battery call at the 6000 block of South Peoria at 3:45 a.m."

These are the images and messages that residents of my community have had to deal with for decades. Even when community residents are working hard to combat negative stereotypes and narratives, their efforts can be quickly negated by local and national media. The same weekend that this headline ran in the *Sun-Times,* our community held our annual Englewood Arts Festival at Hamilton Park, where hundreds of residents celebrated the beauty in our community and had a *truly* good day. However, stereotypes like that misleading headline are ones that residents of Englewood and other inner-city communities have to fight on a consistent basis. The result of this battle is often that the greater public and many of the residents of the community begin to believe the singular narrative portrayed. They begin to believe, even with the positive things happening in their communities, the places they live *are* God forsaken—places to try to escape rather than to expect to thrive.

Like Jeremiah's letter, this book is a prophetic work from a fellow exile to you. I want you to hear the voices in my neighborhood. I want you to meet some of the amazing people who have helped me to realize that God has not forsaken Englewood or any other place in the world. As a matter of fact, we read clearly and directly in the Bible that God has promised never to forsake us. If this is the truth, yet there are communities that deal with greater ills and injustices, we must ask ourselves who *has* forsaken these places.

CHURCH FORSAKEN

Jon Fuller, while director of the Overseas Missionary Fellowship, said, "There are no God-forsaken places, just church-forsaken places."[4] While he was speaking of the church being absent in some of the remotest places in the world, I echo that sentiment for the neglected neighborhoods in cities right here in America. Don't get me wrong: there is no shortage of established church buildings or new congregations being planted in these communities. However, there is a shortage of community ownership and genuine church partnership resulting in community transformation. The church often exists in these communities either as fortresses built to keep the struggles of the community on the outside or as patronizing social-service entities prescribing answers for a community without ever listening.

This book offers a collection of stories and theological insights that come from over a decade of listening and partnering with the residents of the Greater Englewood community on the South Side of Chicago. It is an opportunity to hear our stories so that you too can see why it is imperative that local churches no longer forsake in presence or in practice the places where they reside.

The book is divided into seven church-forsaken practices based on insights from Jeremiah 29:4-7, 11. This first practice addresses how churches have forsaken our God-given *position* and fled or set ourselves up as fortresses in our communities. Practice two reveals that we have strayed far away from God's original *process* of transformation, which hinges on us being with one another. This process is embodied perfectly through the incarnational presence of God who, according to John 1:14, "became flesh and blood, and moved into the neighborhood" (*The Message*) in the person of Jesus. Practice three contends that many local churches have forsaken God's original *plan* to care about the whole person by caring primarily for the "soul." Practice four exposes that we have forsaken God's directive to care for every *place* by disinvesting and neglecting certain neighborhoods. Practice five addresses the fact that we have forsaken God's *people* by abandoning relationships, stereotyping, and jumping to false conclusions about one another. Practice six explains how we have forsaken the original *purpose* for the church, which is to be transformative representatives in the world by loving God and loving people. Finally, practice seven challenges us to see that we have forsaken the original *perspective* of the church, which sees the fullness of humanity and reflection of divinity in every person and place. We have been promised that no place is God forsaken. If we reconnect to these practices, which mirror God, I believe there could be no church-forsaken places either.

RETURN TO PREVIOUSLY FORSAKEN PLACES

THE CHURCH-FORSAKEN PROCESS

Build houses and live in them.

JEREMIAH 29:5

*I can reach my peak in Chicago cuz that's where
I was planted and where I can continue to grow.*

CHANCE THE RAPPER

*A prophet has little honor in his hometown, among
his relatives, on the streets he played in as a child.*

MARK 6:4 (THE MESSAGE)

CHAPTER ONE

WELCOME HOME

As I unpacked my U-Haul truck at my mom's house, I felt a deep pit in my stomach, wondering how I ended up back here. Just months earlier I had been gripped with fear when I received the call telling me that my mom had suffered a stroke while teaching her pre-kindergarten class. I knew it was the right decision to come back to Chicago after graduating from Tuskegee University, but that feeling did not remove the frustration of finally making it out of the inner city just to find myself back again. I am no stranger to moving: I have lived all over the South Side of Chicago and even did a short stint in the south suburb of Robbins. It was difficult to feel at home when coming back to Chicago during my college years because my mom moved to a different house just about every year while I was away. Regardless of how much we moved I always considered myself an Englewood resident. That is because the place I called home was my grandma Thelma's house on the 6400 block of South Wolcott in West Englewood. Although the house is empty now, I have many memories of block parties, games of tag, and long bike rides up and down the surrounding blocks. Whenever my mom and I fell on hard times, we found ourselves back on this block with the woman who, although not an actual relation, graciously took us in at points when we were homeless.

Despite my conflicted feelings and another unfamiliar home, I had an adopted, six-year-old little brother and a recovering mother. It made sense for me to come home rather than pursue a job somewhere in the south as I had imagined. I wasn't that worried about coming back to Chicago considering I had studied architecture and figured it wouldn't be too difficult to find work in a city known for its world-class architecture. However, I quickly found myself disillusioned with architecture, which made living back home with my mom a big deal. Living there to take care of her and my little brother was one thing, but living there with her taking care of me was another.

Although I was raised in the church, I had only become serious about my Christian faith while in college. I often jokingly tell people that it's hard to move to Alabama and not come back a Christian! In southern states like Alabama entire cities shut down on Sunday because the belief is that they are overwhelmingly Christian. After returning to Chicago in 2002, unsure of what to do with myself, I began working with the youth at Canaan Missionary Baptist Church in the West Englewood community not far from the blocks I frequented as a child. Canaan was a church split from the historic Ebenezer Missionary Baptist Church in the Bronzeville community. I was offered this position for two reasons. First, I had an existing relationship with the teens at the church. My mom had started attending the church in 2000, and most of the kids there were the brothers and sisters of friends I grew up with either at Ebenezer or in the community. They already knew me as Jay. Second, to be honest, no one else wanted the job. I also volunteered to serve at the Diamond Academy, the church's afterschool and summer education program, which worked with youth from the local elementary school.

When I began we had about seven or eight dedicated youth coming to midweek gatherings at Canaan, most of whom were there because their parents were making them come. I entered this position not knowing what I was supposed to do with them and never even having led a formal Bible study. I began by playing a lot of games with them and having pizza nights and lock-ins in the church building. Out of necessity, because I was running out of ideas, I began using our weekly Bible-study time as homework time as well. Many of the students were thankful to be able to receive help with their homework, and even some from the Diamond Academy began to stay for our study times.

This connection of students from the church and the community, although unintentional, was the key to the growth of Canaan's youth ministry. True friendships began to form and we began to travel together to school sporting events and special days. Our bond grew and the students began to invite other friends from the neighborhood to our weekly gatherings. By 2005 we were averaging between sixty and sixty-five students weekly and had formed a collective called "The Fam" with three other South Side youth ministries. These were exciting times. I had become so excited about working with young people that I had gone back to school for a master's degree in education and began teaching in the Chicago public schools.

Much had changed in the three years since my return to Chicago. In 2002, I married my beautiful wife, Micheal, and we had our first daughter, Jasmine, in 2003. Micheal and I had moved into a small apartment in the Bronzeville community near the lakefront and were focusing on our careers and building a future for our family. Micheal was working in business and finance, and I had just begun my career in elementary education. She had been supportive as I worked with the youth at church, but we also started making plans about our long-term future together. Like most college grads, we had dreams of upward mobility and comfort.

MANY ARE CALLED, SOME ARE FORCED

Jeremiah seems to be writing this letter to Israel to exhort them to see with new eyes the place that God has put them. They had already made up in their minds that this was simply a place of banishment, and this mindset would not allow them to see any of the beautiful attributes of Babylon. Don't get me wrong: he is not advocating the proverbial "lemons-to-lemonade" attitude. Jeremiah truly wanted them to begin to see Babylon with new eyes. While they may have never chosen this destination for themselves, and while the events that led up to this exilic event were horrific, it is the place where God placed them during this season. Jeremiah wants them to move from focusing on punishment to forging a purpose. Instead of asking why God would put them there, he wants them to ask where exactly God has placed them and why.

Although this may seem like semantics, these are two very different questions. The former is a complaint that doesn't seek an answer to the question but rather an excuse to leave. The latter seriously seeks understanding about the new place and God's purpose in placing them there. When you seek God in prayer, are you truly looking for answers or just an excuse to disobey? My wife and I had a plan for our lives and were comfortable with the way things were going. We soon found out that when we get comfortable it becomes easier to ignore God's calling on our lives and pursue what we desire. When comfort becomes our ultimate goal in life, sometimes God has to go to drastic measures to remind us of what we have actually been called to do.

It is obvious from Jeremiah's language that the exiles would have never made the decision on their own to settle down in Babylon.

The violent and horrific experience of being conquered, pillaged, and carried into exile was not God's preferred way of dealing with them or executing his will. However, taking them to this place of exile was God's way of gaining their full attention. There are less painful ways to fulfill God's plan through obedience, but when we decide to be defiant or disobedient, God does what needs to be done.

By 2005 the youth ministry at Canaan was in full force. Not only were we still meeting weekly, but through The Fam collective we had created a group of Friday night gatherings at different churches and organizations across the South Side. I had been a part of pioneering a Christian hip-hop group called Out-World, and we had just finished our first album, *Undivided Attention*, and were traveling and performing throughout the United States. I was enjoying teaching school, I loved my wife and daughter, and I was excited about the direction of my life.

Later that year, Lacy Simpson Jr., the senior pastor of Canaan, asked if he could speak with me in his office before the Sunday service. I had a great relationship with him. We didn't always see eye to eye, but he had been supportive of me as a youth leader even when my tactics and methods had seemed unorthodox. As I walked in to his office, I could feel a palpable tension in the air. He sat behind his desk with his intimidatingly stocked library forming a theological backdrop behind him. He looked at me and began by saying what an amazing job I was doing with the youth ministry and that he hoped I realized how appreciative he was that he never had to worry about what was going on with the youth. I was honored by his words. However, for the first time I realized that I had been so enamored with the youth that I had not paid much attention to what was going on with the rest of the church.

The pastor looked at me and said, "I have a serious question to ask of you and I am not looking for an answer. I just want you to think about it."

With a puzzled look I responded, "I'll definitely listen."

His next question surprised me. "Have you ever considered being a pastor?"

I responded with an emphatic "No!" Then I went on to explain that I was more than happy just working with the youth and teaching school.

He reminded me that he only asked me to think about it and not make a decision right then. Although I had made up my mind and had no plans to even consider his question, I told him I would think about it and I made my way out of his office. I later told my wife what he had asked of me, and we both dismissed it as ridiculous and something we didn't need to take seriously at all.

A few months later, in March 2006, the pastor called me back into the office again and asked if I had considered the question he had asked me previously. I told him no and added that I did not have any interest in being the pastor of a church.

However, this time he followed the question by saying, "Well, I wish you would have thought about it because I have accepted the pastorate of a church back home in North Carolina, where my father used to be pastor. I was hoping to appoint you as the pastor of this church because I am going to be leaving next week."

I was astonished and speechless. He looked at me and said, "I am offering you the position today, and if you take it we will announce next week that you are going to be pastor. If you decide not to take the position, then we will make the congregation aware that the doors of the church will be closing and they should find a new church home."

I sat there puzzled and afraid, wondering how I ever found myself in this position. He went on to say, "Go home and talk it over with your wife. Let me know what you decide and we will move forward from there."

That was the longest week of my life. I reached out to some of my closest friends just to pray because I was so confused and afraid. I waited until later in the week to sit down and talk with my wife. I had pretty much made up my mind that this was not a good idea. I had no experience pastoring a congregation. I had not been to seminary or had any formal training. On top of that, I did not even have a desire to do the job. All those factors, in my opinion, made for an easy decision. I sat down to discuss the decision with Michéal, expecting her to be upset, as she was my biggest advocate when I needed to say no to a request. I often referred to her as my "watch dog." However, she too had some time to reflect on the decision. After we talked, she sat quietly for a few minutes then looked at me and said, "You know you have to take the position, right?"

I was confused and upset. "What do you mean I have to take the position? I don't know how to be a pastor!" I yelled.

"I know," she replied, "but think of all of those young people who come to church because of their relationship with you. How many of them would have their world destroyed if you don't accept? Not to mention all our friends and family at the church who would be disappointed that you don't care enough to even give this a try."

I hated to admit it, but she was right. I reluctantly agreed to accept the position, hoping that it would only be for the interim until the church could find someone qualified to be our pastor.

After spending a week experiencing every possible emotion and trying to figure out what was going on in my life, it was time for the big day. The pastor and I had been speaking all week, and he promised to make sure the transition went well and to give me ongoing support as I stepped into this role. We sat in his office that Sunday morning for what felt like forever before he looked up at me and said, "Follow me."

We walked out in front of the congregation prior to our musicians getting started with our worship time. He looked out at the congregation and asked for everyone's attention. I thought it was odd that we were interrupting the beginning of our gathering time, but I assumed he wanted to pray or was just feeling a little more emotional than usual considering the transition that was about to take place. But I could never have imagined what happened next.

He said to the congregation, "Canaan, today is my last Sunday as your pastor."

Many of the congregants looked around confused and shocked.

I was thinking to myself, "Is he really announcing this now?"

He continued, "I know this comes as a surprise to many of you, but I am so glad that God always provides what we need. I am appointing Jonathan as your new pastor. He is more than capable to handle this role. I want you to care for him the way you have for me, support him on this journey, and pray for him daily. Thank you so much for your time."

After he said these words he walked out of the side door of the sanctuary to an already packed truck and drove away! I was left standing all alone in front of the congregation, speechless and completely frozen in place. I could not believe this was happening. This could not be real. I closed my eyes tight, hoping that when I opened them again this would all be a dream. But when I opened them the congregation was still there and in turmoil. I just stood there with no clue what to say.

Thankfully, the chairman of our trustees, Brian Dunn, stood up and said, "Okay, everyone, let's calm down. I know this situation is completely crazy, but I believe we will be okay. We have dealt with some crazy things over the last six years, and if we can endure those, we can endure this. Plus, we need to give this young man a chance. Who knows? He might be exactly what we need."

After his words I felt a little calmer, but I soon realized that our church service had not even begun. Was I expected to deliver a sermon or lead us through the worship? I have never felt more insufficient or ill-equipped in my life than I did in that moment. Like an angel sent by God, Brian looked up and said, "Here is what we're going to do: sing a few songs, pray, take up an offering [well, he is a trustee!], and then we will reconvene again next week after we have some time to figure this all out." He looked at me as if he needed my approval, and I nodded back as if I had actually given it to him. I took my seat in the pulpit behind the lectern, put my head in my hands, and began to weep.

As I have reflected on this experience, I have been able to name it as one of the most difficult and frustrating times in my life. I have also realized that I probably never would have accepted a pastoral position the traditional way. I had already made up my mind that it was an exilic role for me. Although God had been tugging at my heart for years, the pulpit was the last place I wanted to be, and the pastorate was the last job I wanted to do. When we are defiant and disobedient, God turns to alternate means of gaining our attention. While the beginning of my pastoral ministry was unorthodox and frustratingly painful, it is also a reminder of the unrelenting call of God. It is important that we listen when God is speaking to us and that we do not forsake the call of God on our lives. Even more importantly, when God chooses us for a specific place and a specific time, truly there is nothing we can do about it. In the words of Jesus, "Many are called, but few are chosen" (Matthew 22:14). I would add that when we don't listen to the call, some of us are forced!

Although they were building houses and settling down while in exile, Israel had not yet realized their purpose for being there. They were to be God's representatives to the Babylonians while living in the last place on earth they would have chosen to be. It took this major turn of events and dramatic displacement for them to even begin to listen to God's voice. It would have been easy for them to be inwardly focused and only concerned with themselves while in Babylon. However, the directive to "make yourself at home" pushed them to invest in Babylon in the same way they invested in Jerusalem.

THE NEIGHBORS SHOWED UP

This pastoral transition happened the third Sunday in March 2006. The next few months were like a whirlwind. It is hard to remember the countless meetings I attended. I met with church leaders who were trying to help me step into my pastoral role and assist me in understanding the business side of church affairs. I spoke with members of the church who wanted to remind me of their influence on the previous pastor, as well as the amount of money they had poured into the ministry. I also met with members, some of whom had changed my diapers, who wanted to let me know how much they loved me, but they just could not see me as their pastor, so they needed to leave our church. Those conversations were difficult, but I also had family and friends trying to encourage me when I wanted to give up. Although I often didn't want to hear it, they would share the typical Christian encouragements like, "God won't put more on you than you can bear."

Of course, there was one member of the church oblivious to all that was going on: my mom. She was the epitome of a true black-church mother and still is to this day. She was showing up week after week decked out in her Sunday's best. Bright suits and church-lady hats were her norm. She found her way to the second row each week and smiled as I gave what I know were rather underwhelming sermons. But by the huge smile on her face and posture of pride she exuded each Sunday, you would never have guessed they were underwhelming. Her unrelenting belief in my abilities as a pastor and preacher must have rubbed off on me because I wanted nothing more than to feel like I had actually earned one of those smiles and amens I was receiving from her.

Conversely, Michéal was having an even more difficult time than I was. I often think back on the dramatic change this must have been for a young wife and mother who dated an architect, married a teacher, but ended up with a pastor. Now she found herself in the most scrutinized position in the African American church: she was a first lady. She often remarks that one week she was just Michéal and no one paid her much attention, but the next week she was expected to dress immaculately, raise flawless and obedient children, and give biblical counsel to any woman in need. The pressure often made both of us question whether we had made the right decision.

However, I resolved to make both my wife and my mom proud and put my best foot forward on one of the biggest days on the black church calendar: Mother's Day. I could think of no better day to prove to everyone, including myself, that I could handle this responsibility. Anyone who knows anything about African American churches knows that there are three major days on the church calendar where you can expect a larger-than-usual crowd. We call those who only show up for these special days "CME members" because they often only attend Christmas, Mother's Day, and Easter services.

As I prepared myself for my first Mother's Day as pastor of Canaan, I was determined to emulate perfectly the traditional black preaching I had witnessed as a child growing up at Ebenezer M. B. Church. In its heyday Ebenezer boasted a congregation in the thousands and was a safe haven and connection place for a myriad of blacks who had fled to Chicago looking for jobs and escaping the terror of racially motivated lynchings and other abuses happening in the south. From its pulpit, great black preachers had shared moving sermons that granted strength and encouragement to marginalized communities for decades. I was ready to take my place on the shoulders of these great preachers and deliver a sermon that would encourage my congregants, lift up the amazing mothers in our congregation, and prove that I was able to handle the weight of this responsibility. I practiced for weeks in the mirror trying to find the right cadence, the perfect mix of poetry and prose, as well as the perfect key for my closing *whoop* (the term used for the melodic and enthusiastic closing of traditional black preaching). If I wanted to show that I could truly carry my weight, I knew that the closing of this sermon was what would seal the deal. I must have spent hours trying to pen the right words. In my mind, everything was riding on this one sermon, and people would either believe I was ready for this or not.

I woke up on that warm Mother's Day morning and felt like it was going to be a special day. I was brimming with confidence, believing I had put in the work to be prepared for this morning, and all I had to do was trust God to take it from there. I even put on a suit and tie, which is a rarity even today, but I knew I needed to look the part of the traditional black pastor that day. Here I was, twenty-six years old, having been pastor for all of eight weeks, and I was ready to show the world that I could pull this off. People walked into the sanctuary in their nicest suits and finest dresses, with white and red flowers pinned to their lapels. (This is another black church tradition: you wear a white flower if your mother is alive and a red if she is deceased.) The worship service was going beautifully, the music was great, and by sermon time almost every pew was filled to capacity. I thought to myself, "This is exactly how I pictured it."

I stood up from my center seat in the pulpit and made my way to the lectern. I thanked everyone for being there, and then I prayed and asked God to lead me to speak on his behalf and not my own. After ending my prayer I looked up at the congregation, and I could see a young man from the neighborhood walk inside the sanctuary and motion to another young man in the back row to come outside.

Now, I knew both of them: the one in the back row was Dionte, who had been in my youth group for the last few years, and the one beckoning him to come out was his friend who had been to Bible studies before. I decided to step back and allow him to step out quickly, which also gave me a moment to catch my breath before I began. Once he made it to the door, I stepped back up to the lectern and asked everyone to open their Bibles.

Just as I was about to name the passage of Scripture, Dionte stepped onto the front steps of the church and a large group of guys rushed him and begin to beat him violently. I could not believe what I was seeing. I yelled at the top of my lungs, "Somebody help Dionte!" I pointed frantically to the back of the sanctuary, but I was the only one viewing this because I was the only minister in the church and the congregation and ushers were all fixed attentively on me. Once people began to turn around there was a large gasp of disbelief. I saw men all over the sanctuary jump up and run to the steps. Yes, you guessed it: a full-out melee broke out on the front steps of the church on Mother's Day morning!

I took off from the pulpit myself, darting down the side stairs and heading down the side aisle to the door. My mother grabbed me and cried passionately, "No! You are the pastor—you can't go out there!" Her plea was so passionate and heartfelt it stopped me in my tracks. Then she bear-hugged me and would not let me go. I was now forced to watch this unfold from the aisle of the church, facing the door. Mark Yelverton, the chairman of deacons at the time, was a police officer. He was not on duty but realized he needed to do something. He pulled out his badge and yelled, "Police! Everyone, stop this. I said stop this!" It did not matter. Nothing seemed to work. He was pulled into the brawl with everyone else. After a few minutes I saw him emerge from the crowd again and reach his hand into the air. *Bang! Bang!* He fired two shots straight into the sky. Everyone immediately stopped, and the guys took off across Garfield Boulevard and disappeared just as quickly as they had shown up.

After this I broke free and ran to the steps to check on the men. It wasn't until I was able to get out there and help some of them up that I realized how serious a brawl this had been. Almost immediately I heard the sirens and I began to worry. I was unsure how this would play out with the authorities, and I also did not want to add any more drama to an already unbelievable Sunday morning. I hurried and got Dionte and all the brothers back inside the sanctuary. I asked for my deacon to remain outside and talk with the authorities when they showed up. To my surprise, not only did the police show up, but ambulances, fire trucks, and even local news media. This was spiraling out of control.

I called my wife outside and asked her if she would handle the media, just let them know that all was fine, that there had been a small misunderstanding but that everything was settled. I reminded her that we did not need them to come inside. The last thing I wanted in the newspaper the next day was a headline that read, "Church Brawl with Community Residents on Mother's Day Morning." After that I locked the front door and went inside the sanctuary. It was then that the magnitude of the moment actually hit me. As I turned around to enter, I saw mothers, wives, and daughters distraughtly hugging their sons, husbands, and fathers, some gently wiping blood from their lips and brow. Dionte's mother, Tanya, who had been coaxed outside, was inconsolable. At this moment I realized what I had been doing before this whole thing had taken place. I remembered I was the pastor and that everyone in the building was looking for me to provide an answer. Walking back down that aisle was one of the longest and most excruciatingly intimidating walks of my life. As I stepped back into the pulpit and back up to the lectern, I wondered to myself what I was supposed to say. I mean, what could I say? Jesus loves us? Happy Mother's Day? Nothing seemed appropriate, and to this day I only remember saying one line—"Welcome to Canaan Community Church, where guns make the difference!"—which was a play on the church motto that we recited every Sunday.

We were supposed to be the church where *love* makes the difference. I could not reconcile how we had been showing love and yet those young men thought it was fine to interrupt our Sunday morning worship over—as I eventually found out—a missing cellphone. At that opening line, the congregation burst into laughter. I am not exactly sure what I said after that, but I do remember asking, "Why was that okay?" I never preached that great sermon I had worked on for weeks because at that moment it seemed irrelevant.

During the opening plenary session of the 2015 Christian Community Development Association (CCDA) conference in Memphis, Tennessee, Dr. Soong Chan-Rah discussed the typical architectural shape of church buildings. They are often supported by a truss system called a Kruk, which I had learned about while earning my architecture degree. The ability of this design to span from one side of the sanctuary to the other without the help of columns, which block views, made it popular. However, when you invert this design, the top of the sanctuary resembles the hull of a boat. This has become symbolic of God's people being safe in the ark as in the story of Noah.

So, here we were thinking we were safe inside our little ark, clothed in our suits and dresses, and adorned with our little flowers. God quickly reminded us that when it rains in Englewood, it rains on us too. I was so impacted by this moment that I knew our church had to do something different. Delivering a great sermon and proving I could be accepted based on church traditions just didn't seem important anymore. For weeks I had worked to prepare what I thought was the perfect Mother's Day message, but God had a different message to deliver. We were not located in West Englewood to do church as usual. Like the exiles in Babylon, we were placed there to be God's representatives to those around us. It did not matter if this was the last place on earth we would have chosen. We were shown that day that if we were not going to get outside the walls of that building and be kingdom representatives to our neighbors, then God would bring our neighbors inside to us.

WHERE LOVE MAKES THE DIFFERENCE

Not only were the exiles meant to be God's representatives in the last place they would have chosen, they were also forced to live and love alongside people with whom they would have never chosen to be in relationship. Through the difficult circumstance of displacement and disillusionment, the exiles would learn quickly that they needed these Babylonians. How else would they know what crops to plant, what the seasons were like, or even the best places to set up their dwellings. Sometimes loving and trusting relationships are created under difficult circumstances. You don't really know how much you need people you had previously written off until certain situations arise.

A few weeks after everything regarding the Mother's Day incident had blown over, I had the opportunity to sit down with Dionte. I had been in contact with his mother, trying to make sure he was doing well and trying to convince him that retaliation was not the answer. I was worried that the incident might spark a war or further gunplay, which we did not need. As I sat and spoke with them at the house, I was hoping to apologize for how naïve we had been as a congregation and express that we should have been far more aware of who was coming in and out of the sanctuary.

Dionte was one of the first youth from the community to start coming to my Bible study. Although I knew he still had a connection to the streets, he brought many other young people, including his mother, to Canaan. As I began to share with him all I was feeling and beg for his forgiveness, he interrupted me and said, "Jay, I just wanna thank ya'll for what you did for me."

A little confused by the statement, I looked up and asked, "What do you mean?"

He replied quickly, "I don't know no other church that would have had my back like y'all did!"

A little smirk came on his face as he continued and said, "You know I don't necessarily get down with the church thing, but y'all really showed me something that day. I keep telling my boys that it was the church people in they'suits and ties on the steps holding it down, and they can't believe it!"

I was not sure how to respond. All my Christian doctrine and theology led me to believe that there was no way that what had happened was a good thing. Yet as we sat having this conversation, I saw this young man connecting with our church in a genuine manner for the first time. He wanted to come back and personally thank all the men who had protected him, some of whom he did not even know. He also commented that he wanted to start bringing his sisters and little brother to church as well.

He told me, "I know that my family needs this kind of positivity in our lives, and my mom hasn't been able to get them here but I will."

As I listened to him describe his connection to our congregation, all my previous notions of how people connect to the church began to be dismantled. No one had walked this young man down the "Romans Road" of salvation. No one had told him he was a sinner in need of Jesus. But the people of God sacrificed their safety and their own lives in order to save his, and that was having far more impact than the countless Bible studies and sermons he had sat through in the youth group or on Sunday morning. I learned in that moment that it wasn't my well-prepared sermon, the beautiful harmonies of our music ministry, or our perfectly planned worship gathering that connected with him. It was not the youth group trips or the years of homework help. What finally connected was the truth that when things got crazy and he needed help, the church was there for him.

As I sat at that table I realized that while he still had not figured out where he stood with God, this young man had made a clear decision on where he stood with the church because the church had stood with him. Often we are so consumed with convincing people that they need Jesus that we fail to show them how much we need them. As the popular saying goes, "People don't care how much you know, until they know how much you care." I was learning quickly that we needed to think differently about what it means to be the church. One of the most powerful Sunday gatherings we have ever had at Canaan was when Dionte and his mom returned to thank the congregation for their protection and care.

Once they were done I stood up and told our church something I still say to this day: "After listening and learning from this young man, I now realize that we can forget about being successful or saving souls or whatever else we thought we were doing before Mother's Day. What God has revealed to me is that we won't even survive in Englewood until we learn to love all our neighbors the way we love this young man. This is what it means to be the church where love makes the difference."

Everyone shouted, "Amen!" and with that affirmation we began this journey toward becoming a new church—a journey that has taken us places we would have never imagined.

ROLLING DICE AND WINNING TRUST

During our talk I asked Dionte if he had spoken to his friend who had called him out on the steps that Sunday? He replied, "Nah, not yet, and I don't really want to 'cause that whole situation was petty.

I do talk to some of the other guys who were there 'cause they came to apologize when they realized how stupid it was. They are always talking about the church though."

Intrigued by that statement, I asked him, "Really? What are they saying?"

Laughing, he said, "They be like, don't mess with that church on Paulina—they don't play. They got guns in there and everything."

A little embarrassed and still worried about retaliation, I replied, "Yeah, I bet they didn't expect that! Hey, do you think they would want to talk with me?" We looked at each other, smiled, and laughed, agreeing that neither of us thought that would be a good idea.

A couple of weeks later, on a Saturday afternoon, I came to the church to pray and ask for guidance. I had watched the previous pastor lay prostrate at the altar seeking guidance from God. With all that had occurred over the last three months, I was feeling overwhelmed and confused. I had no clue what we were supposed to be doing or what direction our congregation should be moving. While it always seemed a little awkward to me, and I was not excited about lying face down on our church's dirty carpet, I was desperate, so I decided it was worth a try. I prayed earnestly that day for God to show me what I was supposed to be doing and to give me direction.

The events of Mother's Day had shaken me to my core, and I just needed to know that Jesus was still with me. After I was done praying I packed up to head to my car and back home to get ready for Sunday morning. As I got ready to drive back to our new apartment in the South Shore neighborhood, I looked across Garfield Boulevard and saw a large group of young men standing on the 5400 block of South Paulina. I could not tell what was going on, but from a block away I could hear the loud talking and laughing. Something about their exuberance drew me in. I debated whether I should go see what was going on. It had been so easy to hang out when I was working with the youth, but my title of pastor seemed to make everything more complicated. What would they think of me? What was their impression of a pastor? What was their impression of our church, especially after Mother's Day? I sat in my car agonizing over the decision for a few minutes, but I just could not start the car and drive off. Ultimately, I decided to go see what was going on. If we were going to be a new kind of church, then I needed to be a new kind of pastor.

I began walking down the block slowly toward the crowd, and with each step closer and each louder roar of laughter it became clear what was going on. These fellas were gambling, and it seemed to be an exciting game of dice. I walked up to the crowd unassumingly while one brother shook the dice furiously in his hands, slid them smoothly on the ground, and snapped his fingers with confidence. "Gimme my money!" he shouted.

I blended in well as a twenty-six-year-old, wearing my jeans and gym shoes, with my dreadlocks flowing down my neck. I stood there watching this intense game from a few steps away before I walked up to one of the brothers and said timidly, "Hey, what's up? Who's winning out here?"

He looked at me for a second before he responded arrogantly with, "Why? You trying to lose some money?"

I laughed and responded, "I'd have to have some money to lose first."

He looked back at me and said, "I feel that, plus I don't like taking strangers' money."

I said, "Thanks, I appreciate that. Since I don't have any money to lose, how about I at least introduce myself so I won't be a stranger."

He turned around and looked up at my face for the first time. I went on to say, "My name is Jay, and I'm the pastor of the church right up here on Fifty-Fifth."

He looked me up and down as if I was an alien and started laughing. Then he replied, "You ain't no pastor!"

A little surprised by his response, I quickly asked, "Why do you say that?"

He didn't really have an answer but followed up with a few more questions. "You mean to tell me you the pastor of that church on the corner? With the stained-glass windows and the steeple? Like, in charge of the whole church?"

"Yup," I said confidently.

He followed up the statement with another question. "Well, what kind of car you drive?"

I was confused by the question and wasn't quite sure I understood him correctly. He repeated his question, "What kind of car you drive?"

I gave him a confused look and replied, "A Nissan."

He smiled at me and then yelled to the rest of the group, "Hey y'all, this the pastor from the church up there on Fifty-Fifth."

One of the guys responded, "Oh the church where they be beating people up!" And everyone started laughing.

I was a little embarrassed as that was not exactly the reputation I wanted our church to maintain.

He replied, "Nah, Pastor cool though. You see he out here with us while we rolling, and he even say he drive a Nissan."

You may be wondering why what kind of car I drove made any difference in this encounter. Unfortunately, in many inner-city communities, pastors are looked at as crooks and charlatans out for their own personal gain. Some drive expensive cars, wear tailor-made clothing, and live in large homes in communities far away from their church edifices located in these neglected neighborhoods. While this stereotype is overwhelmingly untrue, whenever you see a popular movie taking place in the inner city, the preacher is often portrayed in this manner. Popular television reality shows have further perpetuated this image and made it very difficult for the average pastor in these communities to be considered trustworthy.

The game took a brief pause as some of the brothers came over to where we were standing and started to shake my hand and introduce themselves. I asked them how often they were out here. They told me every weekend, as for many of them this was their main source of income because they just were not able to find work. Many of them had children to take care of, and without a steady source of income they were doing whatever they could to provide for them. Many of them explained that they already had run-ins with the police and some of them had spent time in jail. They reminded me of the hard truth for many black men in our country: "You know, once you get locked up it's like you got a disease or something. Nobody wanna hire you."

It has been proven that the Chicago Police Department terrorized communities like Englewood for decades using ruthless torture to coerce people into confessing to crimes. Hundreds of people who were tortured still remain locked up in Illinois—many convicted solely because of confessions given after beatings, electric shocks, and other methods of torture.[1] Criminologists have proven repeatedly that when communities distrust or view the police as racist and unfair, the police lose their ability to prevent and solve crimes.[2]

However, it's not just police brutality. Chicago's neighborhoods also have been devastated by mass imprisonment. America already has the highest per capita incarceration rate in the world and Chicago's West and South Side communities have incarceration rates often triple the national average. Contrary to popular belief, this is not necessarily because more crime occurs in these neighborhoods."[3] As Dominique Gilliard states in his book *Rethinking Incarceration*,

> Our justice system is fundamentally broken but so is our vision. We are socialized to see entire ethnic groups as being more prone to criminal activity than others. We are trained by this society to believe

that members of certain communities of color will inevitably end up behind bars. After all, many believe that the statistics validate this belief. Today it is predicted that nationwide one in three black males and one in six Hispanic males will be incarcerated in their lifetime. We have come to accept this as natural.[4]

Rolling dice, pitching pennies, and playing cards were legal ways for these brothers to double and sometimes triple the little money they might make from selling welfare benefits or borrowing from their parents or the mother of their children. A few of them were still resorting to illegal activity to make money, but most of them told me they did not enjoy jail and were not trying to find themselves back there. I also heard stories of how police officers had repeatedly come and broken up their games, making them lay face-down on the ground, expecting to find drugs or weapons. Garfield Boulevard was not only the dividing line between two rival gangs but two very different police districts. South of the boulevard where our church is located is the seventh district police, whose headquarters is located in and serves the Englewood and West Englewood communities. On the north side of the boulevard is the ninth district, which is located in Bridgeport, home to many of our city's mayors, and serves both the Bridgeport and Back of the Yards communities. Bridgeport was notorious as a community in which African Americans and other people of color were not especially welcome. As these brothers continued to talk, I was amazed at how open they were and how much they shared of their personal experiences.

Before I realized it, I had been out there for hours and it was getting dark outside. I asked them if I could come back and hang out next week, and they told me I was always welcome. It really felt good. Before I left I needed to ask them one more question because it was truly bothering me.

I said, "Fellas, before I leave, can I ask why you needed to know what kind of car I drive?"

One of them said to me, "We was just feeling you out—most of these pastors out here getting rich off people who can't even pay they bills."

I nodded my head in approval and said, "I'll remember that," then turned to leave.

I walked away that day with far more questions than answers and unsure of what had exactly happened. During our conversation Jesus was not mentioned one time, but for the first time since I had become the pastor of Canaan, I really believed he was present and listening to my prayers.

CROSSING THE BOULEVARD

In exile Israel needed to build houses and settle down. They also needed to cross some societal boundaries and do things they had never done before, if they were going to be obedient to the way God had called them to live in Babylon. However, he never asked them to change who they were. The call was for them to be authentically who God had called them to be. Once they were able to recognize that God placed them in Babylon for this reason, the imperative to build houses would make far more sense.

I spent the entire evening thinking about my time with the brothers on Paulina. It was so refreshing. It reminded me of spending time with the youth of the church and community, eating pizza, hanging out, and just listening to each other's crazy stories. I began to wonder why I had ever hesitated to cross the boulevard in the first place? I had made up in my mind that there was nothing I could learn from those young men, and they would never accept or listen to me either. I had been trying to change my personality to fit into the mold of how a pastor had traditionally looked to me when I was growing up. I did not desire suits and ties but rather jeans and gym shoes. I wore nappy dreadlocks instead of a crisp haircut. I love hip-hop and grew up listening to Wu-Tang Clan instead of Walter Hawkins, and that was exactly what our community needed.

Being with the young men on Paulina showed me that God wanted to use me just the way I was and not the way I thought I needed to be. They helped me begin to change my view of what it meant to be a pastor and the kind of pastor God was calling me to be. As well as changing my view of myself, those young men helped change my view of the community. Although I had been raised in the community and had been working with youth for the last few years, it was not until I listened to these young men's stories that I understood many of the issues they were facing on a daily basis. Hearing their stories and the reasons behind many of their decisions helped me to better understand the struggles of the community and the necessity of the hope that comes from Jesus. Yes, clearly everything was changing, and it was all because I crossed the boulevard.

Father Kelly is the executive director of Precious Blood Ministry of Reconciliation (PBMR), which began in 2000 and is located in the Back of the Yards/New City community about a mile north of where the young men I talked to meet every weekend. The organization also houses the Second Chance Alternative High School. Father Kelly, a white priest not from the community, talked to me about the many years of jail ministry, community renewal, and retreat ministry he engaged in prior to starting PBMR: "I was always looking to fix things. While that work was important, the difference in my ministry now is the long-term presence in the community and the ability to see things from a different perspective."

It seems that what was required for me was the same thing required for Father Kelly. He may not have connected culturally as easily as I did, but he was fully present. He crossed his boulevard as well. He had to transition from being a fixer to a listener. We both learned that we should not make judgments about who the young men in the community were or what they desired out of life. When you meet people where they are and hear their stories your view of them changes. For both Father Kelly and me, relationships changed our views—not only our view of God but our view of the community and ourselves. This all began with the decision to be brave enough to try something different. It began with one step across the boulevard.

CHAPTER TWO

THAT'S NOT MY DREAM

A few weeks after my crossing-the-boulevard conversation, I walked into the kitchen of our small two-bedroom apartment in the South Shore neighborhood. With baby number two on the way, we had moved to a larger apartment but still desired to stay close to the lakefront. I grabbed my wife by the waist in the most delicate manner and whispered in her ear, "Babe, I think God is telling me to move back to Englewood." She froze for a second and then wrapped her arms around mine ever so gently.

I awaited her response, which seemed to take forever but was actually no more than a few seconds. She stopped washing dishes, dried her hands, turned to me and said, "Oh okay, so when are you moving?"

Sort of stunned by the response, I replied quickly, "Well, I hoped my family would come with me!"

The conversation went on from there with statements like, "If God was telling you this, why wasn't I let in on the plan!" and, "I didn't sign up for this. If I would have known it was going to be all this trouble, I would have told you to say no!" Let's just say it did not go the way I envisioned.

After many more conversations on this topic I realized that I was going to have to be creative and careful in my approach with this situation. Since the good-old Christian line "God is leading me . . ." wasn't working, I decided to go another route altogether. We had only been living in our South Shore apartment for about seven months. We lived in a third-floor walkup in a courtyard building with no parking. Some days we would have to walk four or five blocks to get to our apartment because that was the nearest parking we could find. We had moved in November and had already endured a grueling winter in this lakefront community. The temperatures were always two to three degrees colder than the rest of the city and the snowfall was four to five inches greater. Now we were nearing the end of the summer and my wife was about to give birth to our second daughter. The thought of walking blocks in the snowy cold and then up three flights of stairs with two babies was beginning to haunt us both in our sleep. I realized what I needed to do to convince my wife.

I said, "Look, why don't we move to Englewood and get a bigger house that we can afford? No more parking blocks away. No more lakefront air and lake-effect snow in the winter." The prospect of finding a larger house for cheaper in certain neighborhoods of Chicago is pretty much a guarantee. Chicago has been officially declared the most segregated metropolitan area in America, which is causing more attention to be paid to entrenched racial inequalities in our urban areas. Segregation by race in the United States has lessened slightly over the last decade. However, one in four black Americans and one in six Hispanics live in high-poverty neighborhoods, compared to just one in thirteen white Americans.[1]

Although she was intrigued, Michéal replied, "I don't know, Jay. That's not really my dream."

But I said, "Baby, trust me."

A friend of ours was moving out of a house in West Englewood that had been owned by an older couple for decades. It was a nice shotgun-style home with a beautiful flowerbed and an ornate bay window in the front, a spacious yard with a privacy fence in the back, and an extra-large garage because they had owned their own limousine service. They had raised their children and were moving to something smaller.

We took a tour of the house and Michéal agreed, "This is nice!"

I told her in my boisterous game-show host voice, "Yes, this can be all yours if you would just join me in Englewood—the choice is yours!"

Let's just say I'm a pretty convincing guy, and the thought of another winter in South Shore did not sound appealing to her. So we packed up our things and prepared to move before the winter hit.

I wish I could tell you I moved my family back to Englewood because we were so spiritual. I wish I could tell you my wife heard God's voice confirm the call for us to move back to the neighborhood. However, that's just not what happened. We moved out of necessity and a better economic opportunity. I'll never forget that day, but little did I know that it was just the beginning.

RELUCTANT NEWCOMERS

The second lesson for the exiles is that after building houses, they must live in them, or as *The Message* paraphrases it, "make yourselves at home" (Jeremiah 29:5). In other words, this exilic land was to fully become their land. If that was going to happen they needed to put down roots and begin to see the beautiful aspects of Babylon. While God's mind had not changed concerning where they were supposed to live, they needed to understand how they should have been living while in Jerusalem. They are reminded that becoming a part of the fabric of a community is the only way you really begin to care about a place. Jeremiah urges them to make themselves at home in Babylon and to remember that wherever God's people dwell, they are called to care for that place as God's representatives. They had to realize that there is no place on earth that God does not care about.

Jeremiah writes this letter to the exiles because even though they knew why they were exiled and what they should be doing while there, they were still having a hard time recognizing the value of settling down. Even in exile they believed the false prophets who were conveniently telling them that they would only be there for a short time. Jeremiah specifically rebukes these prophets and calls them liars: "For thus says the LORD of hosts, the God of Israel: Do not let the prophets and the diviners who are among you deceive you, and do not listen to the dreams that they dream, for it is a lie that they are prophesying to you in my name; I did not send them, says the LORD" (Jeremiah 29:8-9).

Of course, the report of these prophets was well received because it was the message the exiles wanted to hear. It took Jeremiah's letter to relay the uncomfortable truth and remind them that God had placed them in that geographic location with the expectation that they would make a long-term commitment to the place.

Just because God had called me back to my neighborhood did not mean I had a conversion experience in regard to my feelings about the place. I was still extremely apprehensive about moving my family onto this block. Although the house was nice, there were still parts of the surrounding blocks that made me nervous. There were a number of abandoned properties and vacant lots in the area, and there never seemed to be a time when there were not a lot of people standing around outside. There was gang graffiti on many of the boarded-up windows, and the police presence was often overwhelming and intimidating. There was a playground at the very end of the block at Murray Park, which was known as Derrick Rose's practice court while he was a standout basketball player at Simeon High School.

Because the neighborhood did not have the best reputation for safety, Michéal and I made some unconscious decisions around moving in to the home. I say "unconscious" because we never really discussed any of them but just made decisions based on our own perspective of the block and the community. Michéal was a reluctant newcomer and I was a longtime resident, and even with our different perspectives, we came to the same conclusions about the community. We were moving into the house, but we had not changed our perspective of the neighborhood. We moved our important things in the middle of the night, we set up a lamp in the bay window on a timer so no one would know when we weren't home. We entered only through the rear door after parking in the garage; this would keep people from knowing our patterns.

Although we would never have admitted it, we still believed we were better than everyone else on our block. We had a three-year-old and a three-month-old. We explained to our oldest daughter that they should only play in the backyard, surrounded by the privacy fence. We didn't want them to get tainted by those other neighborhood kids—you know, kids with bad morals, with no guidance at home. We didn't want them to rub off on our kids. In our minds we were just being safe and protecting ourselves from the people who lived there. We happily skipped in and out of the back door of our new house and lived in our own world. We lived on the block for nearly a year and never met anybody.

One night we were coming home from Bible study, heading from the garage to the back door as we had done every night for almost a year. As I was reaching for the screen door, the most piercing blasts I had ever heard rang out. *Bang! Bang! Bang!* It sounded like they were right next to us, so I screamed out, "Get down! Get down!" As soon as they stopped, we ran into the house and stood still for a while. My kids were nervous and crying. My oldest daughter, Jasmine, kept repeating nervously, "Dad, what happened?" It was unreal. My wife, my now four-year-old daughter, and our toddler, who had just barely learned to walk, were now holding each other tightly while petrified on our back steps. Eventually, I made my way to the front and carefully peered out the window of our home, over the top of our timed lamp. All I could see were the piercingly bright lights of police cars and ambulances. They were already here and directly in front of my house. I looked up to the heavens and said, "Really, God? You told me to move back here for this?" However, for the first time I realized we couldn't hide behind our timed lamp and curtains anymore. So I went back to the front window and peered out again. This time I realized it was my next-door neighbor whose house had been shot. I thought, "Oh my goodness, that's too close. I need to find out what happened." I needed to know if we should pack our things and move because I refused to have my family this close to mayhem and trouble.

WHAT OUR NEIGHBORS TAUGHT US

So I opened the front door, which we rarely used, and peeked out. My neighbor on my left side, an older woman in her sixties, was standing outside at her gate. The house to my left was owned by another older couple who had been best friends with the family that previously owned our house. You could tell because the houses were identical down to the flower beds, lampposts in the yard, and ornate bay windows. I figured if I was going to speak to someone, she would be my safest bet. So I walked slowly down my steps and somehow mustered the nerve to say, "Hello, Ma'am?" She responded rather quickly with, "Oh, hey Pastor, how are you?" I did a double-take wondering if she was really talking to me. How did this lady know I was a pastor? I had never spoken to her in my life. I dismissed it because I figured maybe someone had told her or she had seen it on the internet. So I just went on with the conversation and said, "I'm good, but I've been better. How about you?"

She's said, "I know what you mean—this is crazy. Do you know what happened?"

I said, "No, I was coming to ask you."

She said, "Whew, I don't know, baby." Then her demeanor changed and she seemed increasingly worried.

So I asked, "Is everything okay?"

She said, "Oh my God, it is Wednesday. You are just getting home from Bible study. As a matter of fact, you guys should have just been at your door. Is everyone okay?"

Completely stunned, I just looked at her for a few seconds. Before I could respond she chimed right back in. "That must have been so scary. You got those two baby girls in the house. How are Micheal and the girls? Ooh, if this had been Tuesday you would have been home already 'cause you teach school too, right? I see you normally get home about four o'clock every day."

I thought to myself, *How does this lady know my whole life and I don't even know her name?*

Although I never answered any of her questions, she reached her hand over the fence to shake my hand and said, "My name is Mrs. Barbara. I am glad your family is safe, but I still don't know what happened. As a matter of fact, baby, why don't you walk on over and ask them what happened?"

Now, let me paint a picture for you. Remember, Mrs. Barbara's house looked exactly like mine—flower bed, lamppost, and ornate bay windows. The house on the other side, not so much. It was an older wood-and-siding house. The porch was leaning a bit, there was no grass—only dirt—in front, and there were always ten or twelve people on the porch playing dominoes and cards. Get the picture?

So, I looked that way, and said, "You want me to ask them?"

Mrs. Barbara said, "Yeah baby, go ask. They alright."

So I walked over and asked them if they were good. "Hey, guys, everybody alright?"

They looked at me and said, "Yeah, Pastor, we're good. Thanks for asking!"

Frustrated, I threw my hands in the air and wondered to myself, *How does everyone know I am a pastor?*

I figured that was the least of my worries, so I turned back to them quickly. "What happened?" I asked.

"We don't know! We were out here playing cards and someone came across the gangway in the vacant lot across the street and just started shooting the house up."

I was like, "Man, why would they do that?"

They responded, "We don't know. Really. We don't do anything to anyone."

I asked, "How long have you been over here?"

One of the young men, nicknamed Twin because he had an identical twin brother, responded, "We've been here our whole lives. Most of us been here twenty, twenty-five years."

"What?" I asked intently.

"Yeah, we've been here since we were little kids. Don't nobody mess with our block. We been here. We take care of our block."

"Really, what do you mean you take care of it?" I said intrigued.

"Hey Twin, tell him about the car," one of the guys said.

"Yeah, tell me about the car!" I yelled back.

As police officers were searching for stray bullets, one guy was being put in an ambulance on a stretcher. Thankfully he was only grazed. As I focused my attention back on the porch, Twin began to tell me a story of how they protect the block. "Look, Pastor. Nobody mess with our block. There was this guy who was driving up and down the block crazy fast, you know, forty, fifty miles an hour. We don't play that, you know, we got children on the block. We be yelling at him from the porch, 'Hey, slow down! Slow down!

We got kids out here.' He just looked at us like whatever and kept driving. After a while he started doing it more and more, just being disrespectful and reckless."

I said, "Oh, so what'd you do?"

"So we caught him, Pastor."

"You caught him?"

"Yeah, we caught him at the stop sign down there. One guy walked in front of his big-body Chevy Cutlass at the stop sign and told him to slow down. Dude acted all tough because it was only one guy. He jumped out the car and said, 'Man, you better get out of my way before I run you over.' When he got out of the car a bunch of us came jumping out, hopping over fences, and running out of gangways."

My eyes got huge, and I asked, "What happened then?"

"He tried to get back in the car and take off. So we started rocking his car back and forth, side to side, so he couldn't drive."

I said, "No way, what'd y'all do next?"

He said, "We flipped it over." Suddenly all the guys on the porch erupted in laughter and started shaking hands. The confidence and pride was overwhelming.

I took a moment to get over the initial shock of what I had just heard and then I thought to myself, *Wow, you know what? That's not the way I would have handled that situation. But I feel safer than ever now.*

I turned back and yelled into the house at my wife, "Micheál, bring the girls outside and have them meet our neighbors!" She looked out the door slowly and reluctantly stepped out. I quickly yelled, "Hurry, bring them outside so they can meet these fine gentlemen, and let them know they can play out in the front yard. I have no worries. We couldn't possibly make them any safer than these guys just made me feel. They are safer now than when we had them in the backyard."

Of course, this was still a complicated issue that became even more real a few months later when my wife and I found one of the bullets lodged inches away from our front window. However, despite the circumstances, Michéal and I both recognize this day, nearly a year after our actual move-in date, as when we truly moved into Englewood. We learned so much in that one encounter. It was refreshing to know we had caring neighbors who were watching our every move, not to be nosey, but because they cared for us even before they really knew us.

But you know what we learned more than anything else in that moment? We learned what humility looks like. I mean, who the heck did we think we were? We thought living in exile, the place we didn't want to be, meant we needed to transform our house into a fort. We thought we needed to create our own miniature version of Jerusalem. We thought our way of living was the right way, and in turn we needed to keep ourselves from being tainted by our neighbors' corrupt way of living. Man, please! Some of our church members told us that while we weren't home they had been stopped from coming in our gate because our neighbors said they had not been told anyone was coming to visit! I immediately cancelled our security system. Not only did we have neighbors who were watching out for us before they even knew us, but we learned a valuable lesson in leadership that day. Leaders come in many different forms.

While I believe in empowerment and was reading books about the principle, I learned firsthand that day what empowerment looks like. When my neighbors ran into this difficult situation with the disrespectful driver, they handled it completely differently than I would have. I would have called a block club meeting and had us petition for speed bumps, which could have taken months or even years to happen. However, their solution fixed the problem in one day! I learned that empowerment is allowing others to lead even if they choose to lead differently than you would. I believe we often confuse the *right* way to lead with *our* way to lead, but thankfully they are not synonymous. While we no longer live on this block and have moved closer to the church, I will always be thankful to Mrs. Barbara, Twin, the brothers on the porch, and the entire 7200 block of Honore. In one day they taught us what it meant to build a house and settle down.

Jeremiah tells us to not only build a house but to live in it. Loving our neighborhood is just as important as loving our neighbor. It was because of our incorrect perspective on our neighborhood that we made incorrect assumptions about our neighbors. When we allow a single narrative of a neighborhood to form our opinions of its residents, we do a disservice to ourselves and the wonderful neighbors we shut out of our lives. I learned that living in community enriched my life; as a matter of fact, I found myself in community. Once I opened up and got to know my neighbors, I actually felt safer than when I built my home as my little fort. I learned what it means to love your neighbor as you love yourself. Finding myself in community was the greatest gift I could ever receive, and it came on one of the scariest days of our lives, a day when we could have packed up and left out of fear. But instead the Lord revealed to us what it meant to love God and love people: "For God did not give us a spirit of cowardice, but rather a spirit of power and of love and of self-discipline" (2 Timothy 1:7). Not only did we gain valuable insight about ourselves and our lack of humility, but the Lord confirmed that Englewood was exactly where we were supposed to be.

The Message paraphrases the second half of Jeremiah 29:5 as, "Build houses and make yourselves at home." In other words, Israel was going to be there for a while. Things are not going to change just because we move into exile. Things in Englewood were not going to be better just because my family was there. No, the passage reminds us to make ourselves at home. God was not telling me to move in to change everything. Who do I think I am? His command to me was to be a part of exile, not to turn exile into my version of Jerusalem. God was not waiting for me to arrive to begin the process of transformation. The Spirit of God had been present all along. I was just now joining the work. There was far more transformation happening then I realized. However, the longer I live in West Englewood, the more I realize that it is within my own heart that majority of the transformation needs to happen.

DIVERSITY IS A KINGDOM VALUE

In Revelation, we get a picture of what it's going to look like when we glorify God before the throne in heaven. John says,

> After this I looked, and there was a great multitude that no one could count, from every nation, from all tribes and peoples and languages, standing before the throne and before the Lamb, robed in white, with palm branches in their hands. They cried out in a loud voice, saying, "Salvation belongs to our God who is seated on the throne, and to the Lamb!" (Revelation 7:9-10)

It's interesting that when John describes this vision, he doesn't just say, "And there was a great multitude." He makes sure we know that this is a great multitude of every tribe, every nation, and every tongue shouting to the Lord in their own language. The reason I can't go into exile and expect to change everybody to be like me is because diversity is important. God needs people with leaning porches and those with manicured lawns. He needs people with white skin and those with brown skin. He needs people who speak English and those who speak Spanish. He needs all of us to be included because diversity is a kingdom value.

In her book *Bird by Bird*, Anne Lamott states, "You can safely assume that you have created God in your own image, when it turns out that God hates all of the same people you do."[2] Is that how you live? Do you think that if you could just make everyone a little more like you, then God will be pleased? Do you really believe that your life is the definition of godly? Do you think that if everyone lived the way you live and had the things that you have that this would be a better world? Do you believe you're a Christian because of what the Bible says or that you are a Christian because of your culture? There's a difference between cultural norms and kingdom living—this was a lesson I did not learn in seminary but on my block. The way I raised my family wasn't the only way to raise a family. I didn't have it right. I needed to learn that God desires unity not uniformity, and unity requires diversity. You cannot be unified when everybody's the same. That's uniformity. To have unity there must be diversity.

There is so much diversity on my block. We like different music and different food. We use different words to describe the same events. I love it! We don't always agree, but we shouldn't if we are doing life together. How serious are you about diversity? How serious is your church about diversity? Is diversity just the new buzzword or are you serious enough about this kingdom directive to allow a new kind of leadership to emerge? If you continue to build houses only where you are most comfortable and live with those with whom you always see eye to eye, then stop claiming that you value diversity.

PROXIMITY AND PRESENCE

My experience of returning home and moving my family to a community that others are trying to flee has led me to ask a very important question: What does it really mean to love? When Jesus is asked which commandment is the greatest, he replies: "'You shall love the Lord your God with all your heart, and with all your soul, and with all your mind.' This is the greatest and first commandment" (Matthew 22:37-38). To be present with God in every way— emotionally, mentally, physically, socially, and economically—whatever we do, we are to be growing closer to God through those actions.

Then he goes on to say, "And a second is like it: 'You shall love your neighbor as yourself.' On these two commandments hang all the law and the prophets" (Matthew 22:39-40). So what do we desire for ourselves? We desire for God to love us and be present with us. We also desire our friends to be around for us in difficult times and for strangers to at least be in solidarity with us. What we desire for ourselves we should desire for others. That's why all the law and prophets hang on those two commandments. When we become incarnational representations in our neighborhoods, it changes our communities, households, and cities, which in turn changes the world. This holds true whether we focus on one relationship at a time or speak to structures and powers to make large-scale changes. If we truly love each other, we will seek to treat all our neighbors the way we want to be treated. This now seems like common sense to me, but I did not understand what it meant to be present with others until I understood the significance of God being present with us.

At Canaan we are trying to live into our tagline, "The Church Where Love Makes the Difference," which we have found to be a very dangerous statement. *Love* is not a word to be tossed around trivially or used as an alternative for "It's good to see you." We are quick to tell people we love them when we really don't. You can't deeply know how to love people until you have spent some time and built a relationship with them. *Love* is not a buzzword! Christians often tell people we love them before we have ever lived with, listened to, or learned from them. If we are going to be genuine, presence becomes a precursor to love and a foundational principle for ministering to the needs of our neighbors. Even the language used when discussing missions in the church can show our desire to escape proximity and presence. While we must speak of the universal church and our global impact, the church's discussion about responsibility in the world should begin with a focus on local church bodies in specific places.

Discussing our responsibility as the body of Christ all over the world is a necessary dialogue. However, we must also discuss the specific role for a local body in a geographic location. The apostle Paul did not just write to the universal church in his letters. He wrote to specific groups of Christ followers in specific places, dealing with specific sets of issues and needing specific encouragement. He addressed Corinth about desiring special roles in the church, when love is supreme. He wrote to Ephesus about their syncretizing of Artemis worship, a female-dominated religion, with Christianity, thus urging the women to humble themselves and allow the men an opportunity to lead. These are specific issues with specific solutions, which we have often tried to spread like mayonnaise over the entire church. We like to assume that the things we value, the places we live, and the societal lenses through which we see the world don't affect the way we read the Bible. We like to assume that the way we view or understand biblical writing will remain the same no matter whether we live in a rural province in China or in Englewood on the South Side of Chicago. But it does not.

This is why it becomes important for the local church to be concerned with presence, listening to neighbors, and knowing what's going on where they are. We then become God's presence in a place, the tangible representatives of God in our local context. If we are going to represent God's presence in a place, then we have to be aware of the gifts, assets, needs, burdens, sorrows, joys, and so on of that place. We cannot just have a church service once or twice a week; we must be aware of and involved with everything going on around us. This includes knowing what's going on in families, with the schools, on the streets, and with the gangs, and being aware of what injustices are occurring. We stay aware of everything going on around us so that we know how to live as representatives of God's presence for all people—not just those who sit in our chairs in the churches but anyone created in God's image. We are meant to be a reflection of God's presence to everyone. The role of the local church is to be interwoven into the fabric of our communities the way God is interwoven into the fabric of our lives.

The apostle Paul's beautiful imagery of the church as the body of Christ reminds us of our responsibility: "If the whole body were an eye, where would the hearing be? If the whole body were hearing, where would the sense of smell be?" (1 Corinthians 12:17). This is what it means to be a part of a local church: recognizing that while we are a part of a greater body, we also have a specific role informed not only by the Word of God but also by geographic, socioeconomic, and cultural factors as well. The local church is also a greater body, and its individual members make up the various parts that connect in meaningful ways in a specific community. This opportunity for local churches to understand specific nuances and needs make them an integral part of community work, placemaking, and presence.

Unfortunately, in many communities local churches are an afterthought when it comes to community transformation. This has lifted the weight of kingdom work off the local church and put it onto parachurch or not-for-profit organizations. While the work of these organizations is important and necessary, there would be less need for them if the local church were doing its job. Even if the need for parachurch organizations did not decrease, their fundraising needs would decrease because they would become extensions of a local church and connected to those resources. The local church should be known as a community asset and a partner to all the community leaders and organizations that desire to see that community flourish. It is my heart's desire to see greater transformation happen through the church's participation.

When I speak of transformation I don't approach it as this formulaic, guaranteed set of guidelines or rules. I don't believe that it is a guarantee that the surrounding community changes because of the church's community involvement or because we seek to love our neighbors. However, I do believe that when God is involved transformation always happens, though it is not always the transformation we are expecting. True transformation begins when you continue to do the things God has called you to even when the only thing changing is *you*. I have lived and worked in a marginalized community for decades, and the biggest changes have been how I perceive people, how I describe the place I live, and how I protect it and make sure no one negatively portrays it from the outside.

To be honest with you, that is a huge change from where I was before I left Englewood vowing never to return. Not only has there been a dramatic change in my perspective, but there has also been a change in the perspective of my family, friends, and congregation due to my transformation. It is contagious. My mom moved back into the community and some of my congregants did the same. Even my friends from college began to encourage me in the work I was doing. I decided that if the number of shootings in our community never went down or the narrative in the media wasn't changing, I was still going to pray and work there because of the change happening in me. Lamenting the loss of life and the pain I experienced in our community was growing my desire and need for God to hear my prayers. I was learning quickly that true transformation began with me.

Ultimately, proximity and presence are biblical attributes, and no matter where you live they are the best mirrors of God and windows into what the world could look like if we all mirrored God. We have to ask ourselves how we can best change our proximity and presence to those around us, whether our close neighbors or people we have traditionally only been able to relate to from a distance. Jesus reminds us over and over again through his words and actions that unless we come out of our comfort zone and get close to one another, transformation will be out of our grasp. The vulnerability that comes with closer proximity is difficult for all of us. It is not natural to be vulnerable and expose our internal weaknesses and fears. We often only have small circles of people we allow into our lives in this way. I want to affirm this as truth and warn against opening ourselves too soon to too many people. Yet I also want to challenge us to recognize that it is when we enter into genuine relationship and experience—the closeness that comes from vulnerability and conflict—that God promises to dwell with us. When sharing guidelines for handling conflict in the church, Jesus says that where two or three are gathered in his name, he will be in their midst (Matthew 18:20). He is endorsing the messiness of relationship and the difficulty that comes with being close to one another and is at the same time promising to enter into that messiness with us.

STOP GIVING BACK AND START COMING BACK

The narrative of practicing presence throughout history is one of good people picking up and moving to places that have been the most neglected in our society. This is valiant, noble, and necessary. What separates me from that narrative is that I was not moving to some new place but going back to my place as a new person. Returning to a neighborhood, of course, brings very different obstacles and concerns than relocating does. While relocators might not be trusted because they are new to the community, returners might not be trusted because no one understands why they have returned. Especially in neglected neighborhoods, where escape is the mark of success, you are considered either crazy or foolish for returning.

In Luke 8 after Jesus heals a man possessed by a legion of demons by casting them into a herd of nearby pigs, the man immediately desires to leave with Jesus. He had been ostracized, ridiculed, and alienated for many years. He was most likely an embarrassment to his family and unsure if he would even know how to live back in his community, let alone be accepted. Would the people really believe he was healed? Would they always hold his past against him? It would have been much easier for him to leave his community where he had been ostracized, imprisoned, and seen as deranged and dangerous. But Jesus commands him to go back home and declare how much God has done for him. Jesus knew the power of the man's presence back in his own community as someone who had overcome the odds. He sent him back into his place as a monument to God's goodness and a reminder that broken people and relationships can be healed. The call back to church-forsaken places is not just about the reputation of the church but the restoration of communities. When we return to previously forsaken places, especially our own homes, we in turn attempt to do something even Jesus couldn't do.

Not long after his interaction with the possessed man, Jesus had trouble when he traveled back home.

> He returned to his hometown. His disciples came along. On the Sabbath, he gave a lecture in the meeting place. He made a real hit, impressing everyone. "We had no idea he was this good!" they said. "How did he get so wise all of a sudden, get such ability?" But in the next breath they were cutting him down: "He's just a carpenter—Mary's boy. We've known him since he was a kid." (Mark 6:1-3 *The Message*)

No one took him seriously and because of their lack of hope and faith, he had little desire to do miracles there, so he told his disciples, "A prophet has little honor in his hometown, among his relatives, on the streets he played in as a child" (Mark 6:4 *The Message*).

I understand this frustration and admit that returning or remaining home, no matter the community, will have its own set of challenges. At Canaan some of the congregants have known me for a long time. I have lovingly referred to many of them as auntie or uncle for my entire life. There were people who left the church when I took over because they just could not see me as their pastor. Coupled with the consistent questioning—Why come back here after graduating from college? Did you really have to move your family into the community?—it can become increasingly difficult to resist the urge to just do what everyone expects you to do. However, Jesus told us that if we believe in him we would do even greater things than he did because he was going back to the Father (John 14:12). I hold on to this promise dearly in the context of returning home. Jesus was unmotivated to do miraculous work in his hometown because the people refused to see him for who he had become rather than who he was. The demon-possessed man desired to leave rather than return home because he was worried about the same problem.

So for those who feel the call to return to or remain in your communities, I affirm the fear and frustration that comes from being characterized by who you were rather than who you have become. I also want to challenge us to believe the words of Jesus and attempt to do something even Jesus couldn't do: make a huge impact at home. This begins when we go beyond the typical philanthropic notions of *giving* back and push ourselves to the empowering practice of *coming* back. Those of us who come from forsaken places know that giving back of our resources to the communities we come from is considered honorable. Athletes, actors, and artists are known for holding sports camps and benefit concerts and making special appearances in the communities from which they come. While it is noble and often necessary to give of your finances, time, and influence, I want to challenge you to go a step further. You might be called to relocate to a different community, or God might be calling you to return to where you came from. In either case it might not be where you want to go. But wherever you end up, don't just "give back" to the community. Move back and be fully present. Your consistent physical presence in these neglected neighborhoods is truly the greatest resource you can give. When you practice presence in this way, you learn quickly that you will receive far more than you could ever give.

RECONNECT TO THE WHOLE GOSPEL

THE CHURCH-FORSAKEN PLAN

Plant gardens and eat what they produce.

JEREMIAH 29:5

It is time for the church, yes, the whole church, to take the whole gospel on a whole mission to the whole world.

DR. JOHN PERKINS

And why ain't no Whole Foods in the hood, All I see is fast food here, can we eat good?

SHO BARAKA

CHAPTER THREE

CO-OPS, CAFÉS, GARDENS, AND GROCERY STORES

God commands Israel to prioritize even what they are eating in Babylon. It was not enough to know that God chose them. How they cared for the land in which he placed them and the bodies he gave them was just as important. Our physical, emotional, mental, and spiritual needs must all become priorities because they make up our humanity. It was not good enough just to consume what was being produced and distributed. The command to plant gardens was a directive for them to be intimately involved in the process of food creation.

This directive to eat what they planted implied that God still required healthy living habits even in the place they didn't want to be. It further implied that physical fitness, health care, exercise, and safety for vulnerable members in the community were still priorities. Israel had been traumatically uprooted from everything they knew and placed in Babylon against their will. When people find themselves in traumatic situations like these, often the last thing they think about is their physical health. The focus becomes survival. Neglected neighborhoods are often identified by this lack of concern for physical health, marked by harmful food options, poor health statistics, and increased trauma from violence, crime, and poverty. Jeremiah makes sure to attach this directive— Jeremiah 29:5—to the previous one. He assumes that you cannot truly practice presence fully without being concerned about your health and the health of those around you.

FROM CONSUMER TO PRODUCER

After my valuable lessons from my neighbors, I began to understand what it meant not only to build a house but to live in it, and the impact that made on my family. I was eager to see what it would mean to live into the other commands from Jeremiah's letter. Israel is next commanded to plant gardens in exile and eat what they produce. Now, having grown up in the city, I had very little experience growing anything, unless you count the small plants we grew in little Solo cups in elementary school. So I decided to focus more on the second half of the command to eat what was produced in my community. But I quickly realized if I followed this command, I would be consuming a daily diet of snack cakes, Hug juices (which somehow contain no juice), and the ever-popular Flamin' Hot Cheetos topped with ground meat and nacho cheese! Although I enjoyed my share of these unhealthy, yet tasty, treats when I was younger, I realized that if I ate only what was produced in my community, I would be dead by thirty!

However, there was still an abundance of small corner stores in our community, typically owned and operated by individuals who did not live within the community nor represent its cultural and economic demographics. Stores like these can be found on any street, in any area, or in any city deemed a food desert. The Chicago-based Inner-City Muslim Action Network understands the corner-store paradigm and the intersection of race and health and has worked with Greater Englewood residents to demand healthier food.

Once I realized that eating only what was predominantly available was not a viable option, I was quickly reminded that the command was not to just eat what was produced but to plant gardens. This was a directive to be closely involved in what was being created in my community. Remembering our definition of exile as the place you don't want to be, I recognized that I needed to be informed about what was being offered to eat in my community. Although I was living there, I still had the privilege of being able to drive miles to purchase healthy foods for my family. I began by asking my neighbors where they shopped for their groceries and if there were any local stores I should consider. Most responded by telling me how far they had to travel to purchase groceries because of the poor quality of produce, meat, and other grocery staples within our community. I was ashamed that I had not realized that my ability to drive miles to purchase groceries was a privilege, and yet the need to drive that far was an injustice at the same time. I began to ask myself what would it look like if we were able to purchase high-quality food items in our own community? What if the seniors on our block did not have to travel miles outside of our community to gain access to healthy and quality food?

One thing I realized in talking to my neighbors was that their ability to afford healthy food was not the main deterrent in food accessibility. Most of my neighbors were willing to pay if they could actually gain access to high-quality food. Even those who were receiving government assistance in the form of SNAP benefits still agreed they would like to have the option to purchase organic or higher-quality foods even if they made a different choice for budgetary reasons. We put our heads together and thought through some ways we as a community could solve our own problem. Through another church relationship we found out that Trader Joe's and other grocery stores will donate food that is either approaching or slightly past the "best if sold by" date.

A group of residents and church members agreed we should begin by accepting donations from Trader Joe's, but we quickly moved on to inquiring about using our community capital to purchase fresh, quality staples from the store. Our community realized that while this was one solution to our problem, it was not the solution we were looking for. We knew that our residents were willing to pay for fresh food and were not looking for handouts. Our church practices the philosophy of Christian community development, which believes that the empowerment of the most marginalized and outcast is at the heart of God. We believe you should never do for someone what they can do for themselves. There are wonderful food pantries in our community that deal with immediate individual needs, so we decided to start the Five Loaves Food Cooperative to help long-term empowerment.

Each week members of the co-op are able to participate with a one-dollar donation and assistance with pickup, loading, unloading, sorting, and packaging of the groceries. Weekly we travel to the store, receive donations, and purchase groceries. Then we bring it back to the church building, set up our store, and all shop together. Each member is required to participate in the entire process in order to receive their groceries and must make a long-term commitment so that supplemental groceries can be purchased weekly. We chose our name based on the miracle of Christ feeding five thousand with two fish and five loaves. Our co-op believes our small financial investment and willingness to share with one another each week is a miracle in and of itself. Just as the disciples had enough leftovers for themselves, twelve baskets full, we believe if we prioritize one another collectively there will always be enough for everyone.

After five years of watching the co-op grow and shift, members come and go, and people begin to get weary of traveling to Trader

Joe's each week, we began to think how we could continue to provide high-quality food without traveling outside of our community to acquire it. We began the conversation of how we could use our co-op budget and find local vendors from whom to purchase. Our congregation began to pray for God to send us a local vendor who could support our co-op and be an asset to our community.

GROWING AT HOME

One day while riding bikes with my daughters to our neighborhood park I noticed a sight that seemed completely foreign to my eyes, at least in our community. We were riding north under one of the viaducts that travels underneath what used to be a main railway through Englewood. Englewood was a hub for railways and was where many of them met and crossed (which is why the community's original name was Junction Grove). We looked to our left, and there was a full-scale farm right in the middle of the block!

Growing Home's Wood Street Urban Farm opened in 2007 on one of the many vacant lots in our West Englewood community. It is now known as the city's first USDA-certified-organic farm and holds several hoop houses, greenhouses, and a learning garden. Every Thursday in the summer and fall, Growing Home holds a neighborhood market where residents can purchase everything from collard greens to lemon cucumbers. This was an answer to prayer for our little co-op and a welcome sight for our community. We decided as a co-op that we would like to purchase our vegetables from Growing Home since we knew their farm and programs were benefiting members of our own community.

In her book *South Side*, Natalie Moore shares some insights about the work of the Wood Street Farm:

> In 2005, Englewood residents designed a quality of life plan for their neighborhood. The quest to uplift the community via schools, housing and economic development, urban agriculture surfaced as a two-fold

strategy: employment engine and method to increase the availability of fresh produce. That led the nonprofit Growing Home, Inc. to expand its agriculture-based job-training program to Wood Street. The transitional employment is aimed at helping people who were formerly incarcerated, homeless and overcoming substance abuse.[1]

It was truly becoming a community effort we were proud of. Not only were we receiving healthy options but also our capacity to buy was increased because of how we pooled our resources. This not only benefited our co-op members but also our local farm that employed the formerly incarcerated—even some who were related to our co-op members. I was quickly beginning to see the benefit of planting gardens and eating what they produce. My family was intimately involved in what was being produced in our community. Our church was benefiting our community in tangible ways. Most importantly, our community was providing options for ourselves through our own creativity and ability.

A PLACE TO GATHER

As I walked through the front door of the Kusanya Café, a myriad of conversations were happening, "Electric Relaxation" by A Tribe Called Quest was coming through the speakers in the background, and I receive my usual reception, "What's up, Jay?" I walked up to the register and asked for the usual, the Mozz Def (a caprese sandwich with mozzarella and tomatoes on a panini named after the hip-hop artist Yasin Bey, aka Mos Def). This time I also asked for a bowl of broccoli and cheddar soup and a large lemonade. "Oh, so you want that soupa fly?" "Absolutely," I responded.

It is hard to believe how we got to the point where I could walk into a café like this in the heart of Englewood. Nearly five years earlier this awkward-looking white guy with a dirty shirt and ripped jeans came walking into our church with his friend Ms. Corrinn Cobb. She had been coming to our church for a few months because she had heard me rapping at an event and heard me say my church was in Englewood. She was originally from California but had lived in Englewood while doing Mission Year, a yearlong service learning program that allows young Christians ages eighteen to thirty the opportunity to live, serve, and grow in the city for a year. Her friend Phil was also an alum of the same program, so she invited him to Canaan, thinking he too would feel like our church was a good fit because of his love for the community. Both of them became part of the congregation and helped us grow to new levels.

One day Phil came to me and shared that he and a few other residents were dreaming of opening a café in the community. At this point, while there were increased options for healthy food, there were no options for sit-down restaurants. There were very few spaces for residents to sit and gather other than outside the corner stores or at public parks. He shared with me the vision of creating a place where residents from all different backgrounds could come and gather. He posed some interesting questions: What if, instead of sending a mother who is having a difficult time with her children to a parenting class where she is made to feel inadequate, she could sit in the café with another mother and over coffee discuss the tools and practices that she uses with her children? What if there was a place for residents to gather over good food and drinks in a safe and relaxing atmosphere? I was immediately sold. These questions reminded me of Jeremiah's directive to plant gardens. I did not have a green thumb, but I did have a degree in architecture and a congregation who could help this dream become a reality. So we began the journey of planting our next garden.

But bringing this dream to fruition was in no way easy. What should have taken a year or maybe two to complete took nearly five years to get done. I remember the many days of discouragement for the residents who invested their time, effort, and finances to opening the café. People wanted to give up every time another potential location was lost, or an owner decided not to rent it. After months of haggling with the owner of 825 West 69th Street, ultimately he decided that he did not want to rent the space because there was too much work to be done on his end. Frustrated and not desiring to lose another place, Ms. Lauren Duffy, one of the residents (and another Mission Year alum) who has a passion for real-estate justice, agreed to purchase the property and rent the space to the Kusanya Café.

Canaan became the fiscal agent for the café during the construction and build-out. Many of our members helped paint, construct, and build the café from the ground up. The difficulty of this process was a reminder of the structural injustice that happens in forgotten communities all over Chicago. Historically, communities like Englewood, North Lawndale, Roseland, Austin, and others have undergone strategic disinvestment. These once-bustling communities experienced racial and economic demographic changes and saw businesses and residents flee. They have been overlooked by Chicago's signature development programs and have been heavily hit with mass school closings. When residents decide to help themselves, there is often so much resistance and municipal red tape that it seems impossible to get anything done. Between the city ordinances, permits, utility companies, and building inspectors, it felt as if the city did not want this café to open. I learned quickly that we would need faith. It was not easy to be intimately involved in the creation of healthy food options in our community. We had to believe this was what God asked us to do or we would give up.

So when it seemed like there were forces fighting adamantly against us, it was my responsibility to keep encouraging my fellow residents and reminding Phil that this was not just a café, it was the work of the kingdom. We were not only called to plant this garden, but we should expect to eat what it produces. For the first time in a long time I was engaging in activity that truly caused me to need faith. No longer was being a person of faith just churchy lingo, it was a daily activity that sustained the difficult work we were doing. Opening day at the café was amazing. As often as possible when I now schedule a meeting in my community, we meet at the Kusanya Café. It is a wonderful place to gather with neighbors and friends. But it is also a place to gather to remember the faithfulness of God.

A WHOLE COMMUNITY

As you can see, there were many smaller victories that happened before we achieved the celebration pictured at the beginning of the chapter. However, while I was initially skeptical about the entrance of the Whole Foods grocery store into our community, it turned out to be an endeavor which included the whole community. Natalie Moore shares about Whole Foods coming into the Englewood community: "Whole Foods shocked Chicagoans when it announced that it would open an 18,000 square foot store in Englewood. Walter Robb, co-chief executive of Whole Foods, made the announcement in Englewood at Kennedy-King College, one of the city's two-year colleges that has a lauded culinary program."[2] While Moore is correct in saying that Chicagoans were shocked by the announcement, what she and most Chicagoans did not know is that Englewood residents were not shocked at all. Months prior to the announcement, the city was trying to get a feel for what residents wanted in the long-empty vacant land at 63rd and Halsted. In our 2005 quality-of-life plan, we had already established our desire to see a major grocery retailer anchoring the land. Jewel-Osco initially showed interest but later pulled out of the deal, leaving residents frustrated and discouraged.

Prior to the mayor's announcement, I was contacted by Chicago Neighborhood Initiatives (CNI), a real estate development company that partners with the city. Their mission is to strengthen

Chicago-area low- to moderate-income communities by collaborating with neighborhood stakeholders on community development efforts. They have placed Walmart and other anchor stores in neglected neighborhoods with both positive and negative responses. The president, David Doig, reached out to me because he had been informed that Whole Foods was interested in being the anchor store for the new development at 63rd and Halsted. You might be wondering why he reached out to me. It wasn't because I have some special influence or am a major player downtown in city hall. Truth be told, David and his wife, Tami, are good friends I met while traveling to South Africa on a learning excursion.

David is anchored in the principles of Christian community development and has worked on many projects like this in other neglected neighborhoods. He reached out to me because he knew that I was connected to the community residents, and before he placed a Whole Foods in our neighborhood he wanted to know how the community would receive the store. I told him I needed to bring together a few other leaders and stakeholders in the community to have a discussion with him, and then we could go from there. We gathered in the sanctuary of my church with a small group of leaders who, of course, raised quite a few concerns. Residents were worried about the store's high prices and were well aware of its nickname, "Whole Paycheck." Others were afraid it was the first step in pushing out the residents of our community by putting in a store where they would be unable to shop.

Mr. Doig carefully jotted down all the concerns to bring back to the executive staff at Whole Foods, but before he left the residents had one more request. They didn't need David to be the messenger between the community and Whole Foods. They wanted to have a community meeting with him and a representative from Whole Foods so that they could ask their questions directly. It was not the most peaceful community meeting ever held, but both

Whole Foods and CNI recognized that Englewood residents were concerned and desired to be involved in what was being planted in their community.

Whole Foods responded well and held a myriad of community meetings after the announcement was made. Residents had the opportunity to do everything from meeting with employees and residents from the Detroit-area store to choosing the products that would be available in the Englewood store. We were also involved in designing the layout, choosing and designing the décor, and even requesting to have local vendors and entrepreneurs sell their products in the store. So when it was time to open Englewood Square, which also included a new Starbucks and Chipotle (both employing Englewood residents), we decided to do it in grand Englewood style—with a party!

The parking lot was overflowing with Englewood residents and community allies as well as intrigued onlookers. Music was blasting, grills were cooking, and local vendors were passing out samples of their delicacies. As we stood in the parking lot of Englewood's first large-scale, organic, healthy grocery store—and only the second grocery store, period, in the last three decades—it was hard to believe we had made it to this moment. Of course, the journey was not an easy one and was filled with many resident-initiated victories that led to this momentous occasion. It was such a day of celebration, not just because we finally had a healthy food store that recognized our full humanity, but also because we saw it as the culmination of our work. We had taken ownership of our own community and had moved from co-ops to cafés and from gardens to grocery stores. This was not just another grocery-store opening. This was our grocery store from beginning to end, and we knew we were responsible for protecting and sustaining it.

God invites us to be intimately involved in the whole of the life of the community. We cannot be so focused on saving the souls of individuals that we neglect the physical and mental needs in our neighborhoods. While Canaan is not the only reason these developments have occurred in Englewood, none of them would have happened without the participation of the local church. This victory happened through Christians engaged in community transformation. The church's involvement is both desirable and necessary, and we are not supposed to be disconnected from what is going on in our geographic location.

Our church logo was never on any flyer, and I was never a part of any press conference. But I am reminded of the work we have done whenever I enter corner stores that have adjusted their food options or walk down the aisle at Whole Foods and encounter many Englewood residents. Whenever I pick up my box of locally grown groceries from the Five Loaves Co-op or walk through the doors of the Kusanya Café, I am reminded that God is with us and that he truly cares about our whole lives—mental, physical, and spiritual. And if that is the case, then so should the church.

CHAPTER FOUR

WHY SAVING SOULS AIN'T ENOUGH

walked through the gates of Cook County Correctional Center
Division 11 and heard each of the gates slamming behind me. All
of us who were visiting were aggressively hurried onto elevators
after being thoroughly searched and reprimanded for not being in
a straight line or for speaking out of turn. I struggle with being in
this place because I often feel as if I am an inmate even though I
am only a visitor. I was there that day to visit Nick, one of our
youth who was a part of the Diamond Academy afterschool program
that I helped with when I first returned to Chicago. He was the
fourth of our young people I had visited here, and with each of
their cases I became increasingly weary of the trauma associated
with this place.

The Diamond Academy was Canaan's afterschool program focused
on increasing academic outcomes for the young people from our
community and congregation. However, many if not all the youth
connected to this program at one point were a part of the youth
ministry activities at Canaan. Nick was no different than the rest.
He would come to Bible studies, play sports, come to our hip-hop

service on Fridays, and had an altar-call experience like everyone else. We walked with him to help him live like Christ at school, to influence his peers, and to grow spiritually. However, we never addressed the home life, negative surroundings, or education and incarceration systems that had been created to ensnare him as he grew. Like many of the other young people in our program, once he entered high school we began to lose connection with him, and eventually we had to close the Diamond Academy due to lack of funding. Even though Nick had his own spiritual experience with God, there were still physical, mental, and social factors that contributed to him landing in Cook County Jail. Whenever I speak to him, he always admits that he knew what he was doing was wrong, but for some reason he did it anyway. He knows that God is real, but it seemed like no matter what choice he made, it was never the right one.

Nick's story is only one of many stories of young people who come to know God at an early age but do not have proper guidance, accountability, and support as they grow. The more I am in contact with Nick and others like him whom I can only speak to through plate glass and across tables, the more I am reminded that saving souls is not enough. We cannot have people believe that Jesus, who is God in human flesh and knows what we endure, would only be concerned with saving their souls. Practicing presence reminds us that while spiritual health is key, there are other factors to think about and fight against once we enter into long-term loving relationships with one another.

HOW MANY SOULS WERE SAVED?

In exile Israel quickly realizes that their overwhelming focus on their religious practices would not be enough for them to sustain. Jeremiah reminds them that one of the first steps for thriving in exile will be to focus on their physical health. God is not narrowly focused on the spiritual components of their lives but has always held their holistic well-being together, as their spiritual health is inextricably tied to their physical and mental health. The prophet also reminds them it is not their sacrifices to God, observance of the fasting laws, circumcision, or any other religious ritual that will set them apart. They must learn to treat people with honor, respect, and dignity, or their worship practices and attempts to share their religious truths will be useless. This is the same message prophesied in the book of Isaiah nearly a century and a half earlier. In Isaiah 58:1-9, the prophet exhorts the people to break the chains of injustice, get rid of exploitation in the workplace, free the oppressed, cancel debts, share their food with the hungry, invite the homeless poor into their homes, put clothes on the shivering and ill-clad, and be available to their own families. These are the true spiritual practices that God desires.

How many souls were saved? This is the question I often get as I share my story and the story of Canaan's involvement in our neighborhood. I jokingly respond that I wasn't counting souls because I was busy with the physical bodies present. I wonder if God looks at many of our churches today with the same confusion he did with Israel in Isaiah 58? Do we really believe God is pleased when we focus on spiritual needs to the neglect of the physical, mental, and social needs of our neighborhoods? The first chapter of James closes out a discussion on being doers rather than only hearers of God's Word, with a definition of true religion: "Religion that is pure and undefiled before God, the Father, is this: to care for orphans and widows in their distress, and to keep oneself unstained by the world" (James 1:27). True religion in the eyes of God is to seek justice for the social concerns of those on the margins of society, as well as nurturing our spiritual health.

FROM AFTERLIFE TO ETERNAL LIFE

I was raised in church and have a strong love for church culture and traditions, including hymns. I grew up in one of the most historic African American churches in Chicago, Ebenezer Missionary Baptist Church, which is known as the home of gospel music.

Ebenezer M. B. Church has been home to generations of Christians on the South Side of Chicago. Since her first congregation formed in 1902, Ebenezer's prominence in the heart of the Bronzeville community has been unparalleled. During the Great Migration of the 1900s, scores of blacks that transferred to Chicago from the South settled in Bronzeville and made Ebenezer their church home. Throughout the years, Ebenezer developed a reputation as a center for gospel music. Thomas Dorsey, the father of gospel music, introduced his blend of Christian praise and blues at Ebenezer. In 1931 the first modern gospel choir was assembled there.[1]

On the first Sunday of the month, like many other M. B. churches, Ebenezer would participate in the sacrament of communion, which we also called the Lord's Supper. Prior to partaking we would always begin with a time of testimony and singing. Many church members had patented prayers they would recite and signature songs they would sing every month. There were many classics I can remember, like Ms. Marjorie Walker faintly singing, "Blessed assurance, Jesus is mine," and the entire congregation joining in and completely drowning out her voice. Then there was Ms. Finger, the sister of one of the ministers, belting out "Tone the bells, I done got over." However, my favorite was when Sister Alzay Green, who was well into her nineties when I was a child, would slowly rise to her feet and lead the congregation in her favorite hymn:

> Some glad morning when this life is o'er,
> I'll fly away;
> To a home on God's celestial shore,
> I'll fly away.
>
> I'll fly away, Oh Glory
> I'll fly away.

When I die, Hallelujah, by and by,
I'll fly away.[2]

There was such a power in these words it seemed like they took everyone to a euphoric state. I now realize that as a young boy I could not understand what this song must have meant to a ninety-year-old, African American woman. When she sang about flying away, she was not only dreaming of being with Jesus but echoing the sentiments of others who had been victims of extreme oppression in the southern United States and were looking for a place where they could be loved regardless of their race and gender. When Sister Alzay sang, she was not only thinking about her soul resting someday but hopefully her body and mind resting today. Her ability to rise to her feet month after month and raise her feeble voice and lead our congregation means so much more to me when I recognize all that she was hoping to fly away from.

As beautiful as this memory is, it is also a reminder of the broken although justified perspective that many of us have about our Christian responsibility. For many of us, being a Christian is about hunkering down, accepting our lot in life, trying to commit the least amount of personal sin as possible, not making God too angry, and then waiting for the day when we don't have to worry about any of those things anymore. That's why songs like "I'll Fly Away" and "I'm Going Up a Yonder" are such favorites. But when we look closer at the pain and injustice so many experience in the world, we can begin to see how detrimental this incomplete worldview has been to our Christian witness and our ability to join Christ in the present work of reconciliation. When we sing about, dream about, and long for otherworldliness while people are being oppressed, abused, and neglected in this world right in front of us, how can we possibly believe we are bringing honor to God?

The rapper Wyclef Jean, member of the Fugees, laments during one of the interludes in their breakout album *The Score*, "We sit around screaming about an afterlife while they just steal this one." Christians do not believe in an afterlife. We believe in eternal life, which is an ever-present, abundant life with Christ that is without beginning or end. When we begin to long for things to get better someday rather than praying for opportunities to engage with the brokenness of the world today, we have become part of the problem.

Rev. Dr. Leroy Barber, co-founder of the Voices Project, often shares an example of how dangerous this type of thinking can become. During antebellum slavery in the southern United States, it was common for white slave owners to take their black slaves to church with them. The only way this could make sense was for them to separate the spiritual aspects of the slave from the physical. Therefore, slave owners could bring their slaves to church and let them hear how God wanted to save their souls, while at the same time believing fully that they owned their slaves' bodies. Their theology allowed them to believe that the living conditions, food rations, amount of physical labor, and even the liberation of the slave were all matters to be decided by the slave owner. The only thing God was concerned about was the final resting place of their soul.

This theology, although oppressive and hurtful, has somehow been passed down to many people of color and has caused us to forsake a holistic expression of the gospel. The implication is that God has forsaken cultural expression, and the expectation is that we do the same. However, in the biblical narrative we see the church engaging culture, not ignoring or forsaking it.

THE WHOLE CHURCH ON A WHOLE MISSION

The question of the church's relationship to its surrounding culture is a longstanding conversation. Throughout history people of faith have had to figure out how to live out God's mandates amidst a culture not bound by the same mandates. The children of Israel were at times called to completely separate themselves from the culture around them. However, the Christian church was never given a mandate to completely abandon the society. Rather, we are encouraged to be actively engaged in the world but maintain our Christian witness while engaging. This is often referred to as being "in the world, but not of it," which is a paraphrase of Jesus' prayer in John 17.

Dr. John Perkins, co-founder of the Christian Community Development Association, has said, "It is time for . . . the whole church to take a whole gospel on a whole mission to the whole world."[3] Before this can happen we must decide on our relationship to the world in its entirety. It is my position that this world is too complex for us to believe that the church has a singular response or relationship to all of society at all times. This is why the local church expression becomes so important to our understanding of living out John 17.

The church is the body of Christ, made up of followers of Jesus Christ who seek to be his representatives on earth by loving God and loving their neighbor. The body of Christ has unique gifts and power when it physically comes together in the form of a local church. The power is realized through prayer, the working of the Holy Spirit, the ability to act as connector and information hub throughout the community, the ability to develop and disciple leaders, and to speak into the moral dialogue on a community, national, and international level. The gifts of the local church are realized through showing love to their neighbors, by living life and serving with them, by doing justice and loving mercy. The church is unique in its capacity to walk with a person throughout their entire life; it is not limited to a specific age group or demographic. Jesus sends the church out into the neighborhood when he says, "As the Father has sent me, I am sending you" (John 20:21 NIV). He compares his people to salt and light, both of which are agents of change and can be felt wherever they are placed. Wherever the church is present, ultimately the presence of God should be felt.[4]

Theologian John Howard Yoder believed that the church, no matter its attitude toward society, is always affecting culture. While theologians differ on how the church should relate to the surrounding culture, as a proponent of Christian community development I am in support of transformation. Yoder goes on to say that Jesus is the ultimate authority for both church and community. I agree with this statement as well. Where I differ with him is when he states that the community of disciples (the church) has the dual function of affirmation and critique.[5] My issue is not with the church affirming and critiquing, but I believe the church should earn the ability from the surrounding community to do both, building what I call "relationship equity." When the community experiences the local church living with, listening to, and learning from the community, they begin to trust our intentions before sharing our views.

On the other hand, the community in which we minister has every right to critique the church because we have opened ourselves up through our Christian witness to being critiqued. We claim ourselves, as followers of Jesus, to be witnesses to the way, the truth, and the life. We are cities on a hill, lamps on a lamp stand, a peculiar nation, a holy priesthood. In other words, we have willingly put ourselves on display for the world to critique or affirm our own description. The community around us has not asked our opinion and in many cases does not seek our affirmation. We ourselves must live in an authentically transformed way in order to see authentic transformation around us. The way we engage our surrounding culture is to build trust until the community gives us permission to speak.

Theologian Paul Tillich better explains my position on how we are called to engage with a culture that is not seeking our truth:

> The question implied in this chapter is not: What is the Christian message? Rather it is: How shall the message (which is presupposed) be focused for the people of our time? In other words, we are concerned here with the question: How can the gospel be communicated? We are asking: How do we make the message heard and seen and then either rejected or accepted? The question cannot be: How do we communicate the gospel so that others can accept it? For this there is no method.[6]

It becomes imperative that we not force our views, no matter how true, onto the community, especially when they have seen no error in their present views. The whole mission of the church is not to convince people that they are sinners. It is to show them that life is incomplete without the unconditional love of Jesus. If we are to speak in a manner that can result in transformation, we must first live in a way that promotes genuine community and makes people ask questions. Bryant Myers writes in *Walking with the Poor*:

> If the people do not ask questions to which the gospel is the answer, we can no longer just say, "Their hearts were hardened," and walk away feeling good that we have witnessed to the gospel. Instead, we need to get down on our knees and ask God why our life and our work are so unremarkable that they never result in a question relating to what we believe and whom we worship.[7]

The book of Acts tells the stories of ordinary people being compelled by the Holy Spirit to go places and do things they would never choose to do on their own. Ananias is told to tell Saul that Jesus wants to use him. He is a little nervous and tries to remind God that Saul is a murderer. Peter is told to tell Cornelius the Italian centurion that God sees him and wants to use him. Peter is worried because Cornelius is a Gentile, and as a Jew, Peter shouldn't be associating with him.

In her *Overview of the Philosophy of Christian Community Development,* Dr. Bethany Harris outlines the stories of the first three times the gospel is presented in the Bible.[8] They are stories of total reliance on the power of the Spirit. In Acts 2, Peter gives a riveting sermon where he lays out the entire gospel story and calls those listening to believe in Christ. What gave Peter the right to speak into these people's lives? They did! The disciples began speaking in other tongues and telling of God's goodness so that everyone could understand, and the people asked how this was possible. The disciples were behaving in such a way that those around them were curious. So we see that as the disciples were together in the community, the Holy Spirit began to move, and because of the power of the Spirit those around them began to ask questions. Peter responds to the question and shows that cultural engagement leads to spiritual connection.

In Acts 3, Peter and John are taking their daily walk to the temple to pray, and they come upon a man begging, who was carried and placed at the Beautiful Gate every day. I believe both of them were doing what they do every day, so this is probably not the first time they have met. However, this day Peter says he does not have any money to give him, but what he does have he will give: "In the name of Jesus Christ of Nazareth, walk" (Acts 3:6). After Peter heals the crippled beggar, the crowd gathers and is confused, wondering how this is possible. Peter again finds himself having to explain what is going on, and he begins to share the gospel message. Once again the disciples are in the community, the Spirit moves, the people ask questions, and the gospel is the answer.

The third time the gospel is preached is in Acts 6, where Stephen has been arrested and brought before the Sanhedrin. He was arrested because he did great wonders and signs out in the community. While on trial he is asked a question about the validity of what is being said about him in the community. Stephen responds to the question with his sermon about Christ. Again the disciples are in the community, the Spirit moves, a question is asked, and the gospel is the answer. My philosophy of ministry and my belief that the church should build equity from the community in order to move toward transformation are supported by this pattern. We should live in such a way that our communities and surrounding culture cannot help but ask questions to which the gospel is the answer.

There was a young man named Herbert Hill who became a good friend of mine and started hanging around Canaan. He was well known in the community, and though he had a few issues with drugs and alcohol, he was known as a very nice guy. He would stop by randomly to speak to me and would say he liked that the church seemed to always be open. He would say whenever he walked past Canaan not only were the lights on but people were playing football outside, and lots of folks were always coming in and out. He told me seeing the way people flocked to the building made him want to know what we had going on in there. After a few months of these kinds of interactions, Herbert asked me if he could hang around Canaan more often because he had been getting in a bit of trouble with the police and needed to spend his time more productively. I told him the doors of the church were always open to him, literally, and all he had to do was show up.

After a while he was hanging around so much, we offered him a security position at the church, even though he didn't ask for it. He accepted and was faithful at looking out for our congregation and my family as well. His service earned him the nickname "Top Flight Security," taken from the popular African American movie *Friday after Next,* one of many sequels to *Friday,* written by Ice Cube. A few years ago, when we had a huge blizzard in Chicago, I received a phone call from Herbert telling me to look out my window. When I peered through the blinds, there he was, standing in snow above his waist, waving at my wife and me, while beginning to shovel our walkway.

Herbert worked with us for a little over a year, and we experienced lots of ups and downs. We checked him into a rehab facility and he left early. We helped him with housing and he was evicted. However, we never stopped loving him, and when he returned his security jacket awaited him. Unfortunately, for reasons beyond our control, he suddenly moved to Baltimore. For the first few months he was gone I would often speak with him over the phone. One evening as we were talking, he began to tell me about some of the churches he had visited since moving, and he asked me a very poignant question: "Why is your church so different? When I came to Canaan you guys just welcomed me with open arms. I know I didn't have it all together, but you welcomed me in regardless. It seems like the churches I visit now want me to change before they even get to know me." I took this opportunity after all these years to share with him our understanding of the unconditional love of Christ. Herbert had been a part of numerous services at Canaan and heard dozens of sermons. But it was this moment on the phone where Herbert decided to be a follower of Jesus. None of this happened until he was ready to ask me that crucial question.

Not long after that call I lost touch with him and we did not speak for almost two years. I recently found out that Herbert passed away from an asthma attack while at work in Baltimore. When I was reunited with his family, they told me how much his life had completely changed. He had stopped using drugs, was a faithful church member, and was engaged to be married when he passed away suddenly. I was moved to tears after hearing the way the Spirit of God had done a serious work in Herbert's life—so much so that those around him could visibly tell the difference. It was exciting to know that our love for Herbert over the years and our desire for him to be a part of our community contributed to the work God did in his life. The Spirit of God was able to work through our unconditional love, prompting him to ask the question to which the gospel could be the answer.

Practicing presence is not a quick process, nor does it necessarily guarantee the results we expect. I also do not assume it is the only way that people come to know Jesus. However, it is the best way to exemplify the unconditional love of Christ to all people because it has a dual impact. Our congregation and my family learned so much through the sacrificial life of Herbert Hill. If local churches can trust the process of presence and not try to anticipate or dictate results for God, the process of transformation can be a reciprocal endeavor. Practicing presence in neglected neighborhoods will allow the local church to be transformed just as much as those we seek to love unconditionally.

THE WHOLE GOSPEL TO THE WHOLE WORLD

While I appreciate their scholarship and value their contributions, I have one major critique of all the theologians I have mentioned thus far: none of them speak from the perspective of the disenfranchised. They are conveniently able to funnel their theologies of church and culture through lenses of privilege. Each assumes that the individuals who make up the church are able to choose their position as it relates to the surrounding culture. How different is the conversation when those who make up the church are marginalized by the society and therefore have their cultural relationship prescribed for them? In his book *Jesus and the Disinherited*, Howard Thurman states, "Too often the price exacted by society for security and respectability is that the Christian movement in its formal expression must be on the side of the strong against the weak."[9]

When Pastors Charles and Florence Mugishe, the founders and directors of Africa New Life Ministries, returned to Rwanda after studying in the United States, they saw the post-genocide need for holistic ministry. Their organization began as a child-sponsorship ministry for students in elementary through high school. Pastor Charles, who studied at Multnomah Seminary in Portland, Oregon, returned to share the gospel of Christ and plant a church in Rwanda. While doing great evangelistic work, he noticed something that bothered him to his core. He watched people coming week after week to give their lives to Christ. They would raise their hands and repeat the sinner's prayer but then leave that place with no food, no water, no shelter, and no hope for today. He was addressing the problem of where they would spend eternity but not addressing the problem of where they would spend the night!

So New Life Bible Church grew into Africa New Life Ministries. Their Kigali Dream Center houses New Life Bible Church, Africa College of Theology, Dream Medical Center, Dream Coffee Shop, Dream Ministry Center (which includes Dream Christian Academy, Dream Tutoring, Dream Daycare, Dream Beauty Academy, Dream Sewing Classes), and other vocational training. And this is just one of four sites in Rwanda. Pastors Charles and Florence recognized that as needs arise, the whole gospel of Christ brings good news in every area. They call this presenting the gospel with both hands— one hand being the spiritual needs and the other the physical needs. We are able to lift one another when we use both hands together. They give me hope that returning to your community to follow God's call can lead to holistic transformation. But while there is much good work happening in their ministry, even they must be careful not to assume they know what's best for the communities they serve.

When we speak of the church's relationship to its community, what assumptions are we making? We must not assume that the church has the ability to engage its surrounding neighborhood in a healthy way, if it so chooses. This assumes that both church and community are on an even social, political, and economic foundation.

But for those living in neglected neighborhoods, this foundation is nonexistent, which often creates an uneven power dynamic when the church gets involved. When the church sets itself up on the side of the powerful, we alienate the very people we say we love. Thurman states, "It will lead us to counsel either the culture or the church to ask the question what should we do for those whose need is greater than ours, rather than asking what does our religion offer us to meet our own needs."[10] To hear congregants speak as if they only have assets and no deficits feels patronizing to those who have been neglected. It comes across as condescending to act as if we only come to serve and have nothing to receive from the community. We must be careful not to look at the relationship between church and community through rose-colored glasses. We must constantly ask if our church is sharing the whole gospel, a gospel that uplifts the marginalized. Let us, like the early Christians, even in our discussions and theological theories, remember the poor. Otherwise we are at risk of neglecting to share the whole good news of the gospel. Any gospel message that is not good news to everyone is not the gospel at all.

While this book focuses on local church expressions, we must remain aware of the church's responsibility to the various cultures of the world. This thought often haunts me as a local parish pastor because engaging my local context alone feels overwhelming. However, if I am going to live into the holistic nature of the good news, I must be in touch with the issues of the world and the church's relationship to suffering everywhere. In 2012 I had the opportunity to take a class through Northern Theological Seminary called "Experiencing Africa and the Gospel" with Dr. Wayne Gordon, pastor of Lawndale Community Church. The course objectives were to help students understand the complexities of poverty, racism, injustice, and other factors that have contributed to the under-resourced communities all over the world. It was an eye opener for me. There were so many similarities between the rugged paths of Kibera, the largest slum in Kenya, and the streets of the South Side of Chicago. I saw men sitting on the side of the road on crates, panhandlers and street hustlers on every block. There was loud hip-hop music blasting out of the barber shops and salons and groups of individuals standing on the corners conversing loudly.

It hit me that all the behaviors that are frowned on in American society are everyday activities in Kenya. Everything felt so natural, and my feelings about my own community were affirmed. The people in my community are not strange, lazy, and loud; we are of African descent and resilient! I was reminded that all the issues faced by Americans living in neglected neighborhoods are the same as those faced by the marginalized across the world. Although the local church has a responsibility to its surrounding community, it also has a responsibility to the entire world. I have made friends with pastors in Kenya and Ethiopia and continue to pray with and for them. We help each other think of creative ways to engage our communities and the broader surrounding culture. No matter where they live, those on the margins must recognize fear, deception, and hatred for what they are.[11] Then they must learn how to destroy these powers or render themselves immune to their domination through the power of love and the beauty of mutually transforming relationships.

Ultimately, transformation cannot be unidirectional. The church and the community must engage with one another to experience mutual transformation. In doing so they will find what they can learn from each other as they grow in an interconnected manner. This will often expose brokenness on both sides as well as bless the beauty that each brings. True transformation comes from authentic relationships, not the bashing of one another's views and experiences. This is a picture of the incarnational love of Jesus Christ, who entered into our brokenness and blessed us in order to see true transformation happen:

The Word became flesh and blood, and moved into the neighborhood. We saw the glory with our own eyes, the one-of-a-kind glory, like Father, like Son, Generous inside and out, true from start to finish. (John 1:14 *The Message*)

When Jesus moved into the neighborhood, we got a close-up view of his generosity. This becomes the task of the church as it relates to the surrounding community. We must be willing to engage the culture on its terms so that God's glory might be revealed to all. And although we often forget, that "all" includes us!

PRACTICE FOUR

REESTABLISH THE VALUE OF PLACE

THE CHURCH-FORSAKEN PLACE

Take wives and have sons and daughters; take wives for your sons, and give your daughters in marriage, that they may bear sons and daughters; multiply there, and do not decrease.

JEREMIAH 29:6

I got my city doing front flips when every father, rapper, mayor jump ship. I guess that's why we call it where I stay, clean up the streets so my daughter can have some place to play.

CHANCE THE RAPPER

If a church does not attend to its geography, whatever is going on inside it is vapid and superficial.

DR. WILLIE JENNINGS

CHAPTER FIVE

GOD, HAVE YOU LOOKED OUT YOUR WINDOW?

became quite fond of the Jeremiah 29 passage because it seemed to make sense of the direction my life was going. I began to take it seriously and wanted to know if it applied further to my life. It was hard to believe how directly it was speaking to my family. I wish I could say that as I continued to read and study the passage it encouraged me, but actually the opposite happened. I understood that God not only wanted his people to invest in exilic real estate but to live in exile themselves, not only to increase food access in Babylon but to eat what was being produced there. The next part of Jeremiah's letter states that God does not want us just to live and eat in exile but to increase there. We are told to create generational value for the place we don't want to be. We are to get married and have exilic children, then marry off our exilic children to other exilic children, so that we can have exilic grandchildren. Two commands follow: multiply there and do not decrease.

I read this part over and over again, hoping I had read incorrectly. After the fourteenth or fifteenth reading, I slammed my Bible shut, looked up to heaven and said, "God, I was with you until you started talking about my daughters!" I got up from my living room table and went to the window, pointed to the corner of my block, and screamed, "God, have you looked out your window lately? You cannot be seriously thinking that I am supposed to give my beautiful daughters to these knuckleheads. Look at them standing on the corner, pants at their ankles, with no ambition, no respect, and no business being anywhere near my daughters!" As I sat in my window confused and frustrated, I did what any husband at his wits' end would do: I went to ask my wife.

REMEMBER WHERE YOU'RE FROM

I have always valued being a man of integrity, for I believe that character is the bedrock of faith. It is because of character and integrity that we trust God's promises and commands. So as I prepared to one day share this passage of Scripture as one that has run parallel to my life, it was important to me to live out what was being said. I went to Michéal and said, "I am really having trouble with a certain part of this passage. I think it could be powerful, but I don't like what God is asking me to do."

She looked at me with real concern in her eyes. I must have looked deeply troubled because in a soft, comforting voice she replied, "Well, what does it say?" I read through it and then explained that I felt like God was telling me to take my daughters and marry them off to young men from my community. While there were probably a few outliers, the majority of the young men I saw standing around our community I did not want anywhere near my daughters. Once I was done pleading my case, my wife looked at me intently. The concern in her eyes turned to a scowl of disgust and the soft, comforting voice shifted to a boisterous, attitude-filled tone. She shook her head and said, "You're so stupid."

Appalled by the response, I immediately became defensive. Before she could even finish her sentence, I asked how she could respond so insensitively when I was going through a crisis of faith. I reminded her that I had carefully studied the passage and looked at the context in which it was written. I knew what was going on geographically, structurally, and culturally in the passage and was able to contextualize it for my situation. She looked at me and said, "All of that is nice, but you still don't get it."

By now I was getting upset because I felt belittled and not heard, so I raised my voice and said angrily, "Oh, so you know how to properly exegete a passage of Scripture? Are you a biblical scholar now? Maybe I should just let you preach the sermons from here on out!" I held my Bible out to her and said smugly, "Okay, Mrs. Theologian, since you know everything, why don't you just tell me what the passage is saying and how I can make sense of it in today's society? I'll wait!"

I stood there with folded arms, thinking I had completely shut down anything she could say. No sooner than I finished my statement, Michéal looked me in the eyes, pressed her pointer finger right into the middle of my forehead and said four words I will never forget: "Stupid, you're from Englewood!"

I forgot. Even as someone born and raised on the South Side with roots in this same community, I had fallen prey to the notion that all the young people in my community were the same and that I should see them the way all of society does: not one of them was good enough for my daughters. Although I had made my home here, I was not sold on making a generational investment. However, with just four words in the motherly tone that only Michéal Newman-Brooks can invoke, I realized that I had forgotten. I had forgotten that not every young person in my community was evil or a bad influence. I had forgotten that there was a time when I was standing outside of some other dad's window wearing a pair of Girbaud jeans two sizes too big, an oversized Wu-Tang Clan shirt, large Koss headphones plugged into my Walkman, and carrying a backpack full of spray-paint cans. I am sure that there were plenty of fathers looking out their windows at me asking the same question: Really, God? I had forgotten that while I was a little rough around the edges and had a lot to learn about how to treat someone I cared for, God was in the business of transforming me from the inside out and not the outside in.

In other words, my outer appearance wasn't the problem. The problem was the need for the inner change that can only come from a genuine connection to God and from the freedom found in following Jesus into a lifestyle of love, grace, justice, and peace. I had forgotten! While these were all great reminders of who God is and how much God loves us, the greatest moment of learning came when I began to discern what this verse meant for my family and me. If we were to increase here and the value of our exilic location was to grow, then there were some serious implications for our responsibility to our fellow exiles.

IT'S ON US

I sat in my window that evening thinking about what had transpired and how that conversation had taken an unexpected turn. I was newly amazed at how much God loves us and how quickly we forget where God has brought us from and how far we still have to go in our personal development and discipleship. I wondered about what my response should be as a representative of the God who is always transforming people. Am I just supposed to pray, sit back, and wait for the transformation to happen in my community and in my neighbors? I began to hear God inviting me and his entire church into the mysterious work of transformation and reconciliation. I sat up in my chair and yelled, "It's on us!" God was not expecting transformation to happen in our community or anywhere else in the world without the participation of his church. We would join him in the work.

I realized that if I was going to make sure there was a good crop of young men in the community for my daughters to choose from, then I needed to stop talking *about* them from my window and start talking *to* them out on the street. I knew what it was like to grow up in a single-parent household and to desire male mentorship and yet wind up left to your own devices when trying to figure out what it meant to be a man. I knew what it was like to walk the streets of Englewood alone as a teenager, and I knew the alluring appeal of gang life. I understood these realities, and while I could not always understand the stories of others, I could make myself available to listen.

So I began to get to know the young men and women in the community who I had such strong feelings about. Our church partnered with the Cook County Juvenile Detention Center's Faith-Based Recidivism Reduction Initiative. We began to walk alongside court-involved young people in our community, having them assigned to our church for mentorship and different life experiences, rather than being shipped back to the juvenile jail for every little offense. I began to walk with young people in the community, some of whom had been part of our Diamond Academy afterschool program. One student, Tommie Williams, had come to our program as a young kid with some rough edges. He was often upset and would get into trouble at school for his temper and inability to control his anger. One day after programming he decided to "borrow" the snare drum from the church set. He connected it to a shoestring, hung it from his neck, and marched happily around the neighborhood. Once we figured out that he was the one who had taken it, we discussed with him why it hurt us that he stole the drum and how it affected us. Ultimately, we kept him in the program and our church continued to love him and even offered to give him drum lessons. He remained in our program and we made sure to keep up with him all through high school and college, even providing financial and moral support. A decade later we were able to celebrate with him and his family at his graduation from Southern Illinois University at Carbondale.

Conversely, for others we ended up having to make regular visits to Cook County Jail. We have walked with young couples through teen pregnancies and encouraged them to keep moving forward despite whatever setbacks may come. Reconciliation becomes a concrete process when you are trying to help teenage parents work through their differences when raising children. One of the ministers at our church, Cheryl Benson, had been a teenage mother herself and felt a special calling to work with young single mothers. From there began Mothers Achieving the Master's Agenda (MAMA), a ministry focused on walking with young mothers who want to continue moving forward in their lives and faith even after an unplanned pregnancy. It did not matter which direction their lives were heading, we understood that God was in the business of reconciliation. We see all these young people as God's creation, and we are invited to participate in the process no matter how long or where it may take us.

Suddenly, certain Scriptures that had felt abstract before began to make concrete sense to me, such as:

> From now on, therefore, we regard no one from a human point of view; even though we once knew Christ from a human point of view, we know him no longer in that way. So if anyone is in Christ, there is a new creation: everything old has passed away; see, everything has become new! All this is from God, who reconciled us to himself through Christ, and has given us the ministry of reconciliation; that is, in Christ God was reconciling the world to himself, not counting

their trespasses against them, and entrusting the message of reconciliation to us. So we are ambassadors for Christ, since God is making his appeal through us; we entreat you on behalf of Christ, be reconciled to God. (2 Corinthians 5:16-20)

This human and divine partnership for reconciliation is hard work and takes lots of patience. We realized how patient God had been with us and how much more would be required of us as a congregation. We were not just talking about faith in God, we were dependent on God as we partnered with him to see transformation happen. We also realized that this work would take a long time. We would be walking with people for years, and still some of them would make the same decisions that previously led them to difficult circumstances. It made sense why God would want us to increase in number here and not to decrease. If we wanted to be a part of transformation and reconciliation in our community, then we would need to be around for a while. Transformation does not happen through individuals alone; it happens through generations of individuals committing to a place, recognizing its value, and instilling that value in the next generation. God was partnering with us to make transformation happen and was reinforcing that transformation was dependent on us. Of course, when I say "us," I am talking about God and his people.

Next time you look out your window and begin to complain about what you see, remember the words of Dr. King: "Prayer is a marvelous and necessary supplement of our feeble efforts, but it is a dangerous substitute."[1] God's plan and desire for transformation is the same no matter our place. There are those who look out their windows and see a different view than the one I saw from mine. You may see big houses with fancy valances and blinds covering up what's going on behind them. The need for transformation and the need to connect to your place is still primary. Even there it's on us. Increase your influence there and do not decrease. God is working through our presence to transform all neglected neighborhoods, even when the neglect is not financial. I am thankful for my wife and her boldness to share those four little words that completely changed the value of my place. When it comes to the value of your place, what might God be saying to you?

CHAPTER SIX

PROMISING PLACE

I spent most of my years as an elementary school teacher focusing on the arts: music, visual art, theater, and dance. However, my first year of teaching was one of my favorites because I had the opportunity to be in a fifth-grade classroom with two other teachers: my fellow classmate, Mr. Treymaine Moore, and our lead teacher, Dr. Mellodie Brown. Mellodie was not only a master teacher but an amazing mentor. She taught us that one of the most important lessons to teach was the five Ws: Who? What? Where? When? Why? She said, "These five little questions are at the center of many of life's most crucial decisions. If we can get students to ask these questions, not only of the narratives they read and write but of the one they are living daily, then we are really teaching them critical-thinking skills." I have never forgotten that insight, and I continue to ask these important questions daily.

We are all writing narratives as we walk through our lives. If we are not careful about what questions we prioritize, we may just perpetuate problematic narratives. Even as a follower of Jesus, called to love unconditionally, I was misguided about the value of the place to which I was called to return. I had applied the five Ws to my life, but in the order in which I prioritized them.

- What does God want me to do?
- Who has God created me to be?
- When am I ready to step into that calling?
- Why would God choose me?
- Where does God want me to be?

Just like many Christians, I was most concerned with what God wanted me to do. The most prominent Christian literature and art focus on calling, purpose, destiny, and gifts. And God is definitely concerned about what we are doing. There are plenty of Scriptures that tell us that our behavior impacts how people see God. Jesus even closes out the first section of his Sermon on the Mount with, "Let your light shine before others, so that they can see your good works and give glory to your Father in heaven" (Matthew 5:16). This question, as well as the other four, is valid and warrants consideration and prayer.

One of the five questions is typically regarded as an afterthought, or maybe only as the result of the answers to the other questions. How often do we begin by asking where God wants us to be? In the biblical narrative, God rarely commands what to do without also saying where to do it. Abraham was told that he would have descendants numbering more than the stars, but first he had to leave and go to the place where God needed him. Each of the prophets was not only given a message but a place in which to share that message. Jesus even gives his disciples specific locations where they will be his witnesses to eventually reach the world.

Somehow our society and our theology have made us believe that we have the right to live wherever we want. Since God's presence is everywhere, we believe we have the right to live anywhere. The problem is that there are very few of us who willingly choose places of exile. Going to some little-known corner of the world might garner some respect and prayer from others, but we are especially not inclined to choose to be uncomfortable if that place happens to be home. Whether home or abroad, we pray about "what" and then feel we have the freedom to decide "where."

The term often used as code language for neglected neighborhoods is *under-resourced*. My issue with this language is that it fails to name the reasons this under-resourcing occurs. Many places in the world are under-resourced because too many of us have neglected to seek God about where we should be. Therefore, we have taken gifts, resources, and relationships meant for these places and moved them to our chosen destinations. I suggest that we begin to prioritize the question of where. As we find this answer and begin to value the places God sends us, the answers to the other questions will emerge. Once we invest in where we have been placed, we grow to love who is there. Our neighbors will in turn grow to love us and help us understand what we should be doing and when it is appropriate for us to begin doing it. As we invest deeper into our place and reflect on the journey, it will begin to make sense as to why we are there. This is true of every place, but especially of our places of exile. This prioritizing of place is a way of practicing presence that I call living at the center of the five Ws.

THE IMPORTANCE OF PLACE IN THE BIBLE

Jeremiah's letter is a reminder to Israel that God has always been concerned with their geographic location and that valuing and understanding their place is a guiding factor in achieving God's will. The reason they find themselves in exile is because of the misuse of the original place they were given and a misunderstanding of what God was doing through the location chosen for them. Once Moses leads the freed slaves out of Egypt they come to a place God has chosen for them, but because of their fear and disobedience God does not allow them to inhabit this place for forty years.

Let's talk about this place God has prepared for them, this little strip of land about the size of New Jersey that I like to call the "Land Between." To understand the relevance of this biblical geography we have to go back and begin with God's promise to Abraham and then move outward to the implications for Israel throughout the Old Testament and then for the church in the New Testament. The Land Between was part of the promise God made to Abram in Genesis 12 and important to the future of God's plan.

> Abraham received his divine call at Haran: "Go from your land, your family, and your father's home to the land I will show you." The Bible records Abraham's journeys but relatively few details along the way. It does preserve illustrations of Abraham's life of faith, later summed up by a remarkable statement in the book of Hebrews: "By faith Abraham, when called to go to a place he would later receive as his inheritance, obeyed and went, even though he did not know where he was going" (Heb 11:8).[1]

It's eye opening to realize that the geographic location of the Land Between informs almost the entire Old Testament narrative. In the summer of 2014 I traveled to Israel-Palestine for three weeks to study the geographical and historical settings of the Bible at Jerusalem University College. I had always pictured the land of the conquests as lush, green, and resourceful, where all the needs of the Israelites would be met. But seeing and experiencing that much of it is arid, dry, and hilly terrain made me realize how incorrect my imagination had been. All the major powers of the region (Egypt, Babylon, and Assyria) knew that the best way to travel, whether for conquest or trade, was through the Land Between. The geographical features were perfect for traveling. There were basins or grooves, known as wadis, that collected water during the rainy season. This created land bridges known as ridge routes which served as highways for trade. The most prominent and well-known international trade routes ran right through the center of this region, and it became a funnel point for all who wanted to trade.

The region is referred to as the Fertile Crescent because it is a crescent-shaped area that sits between the coast and the desert and is the most fertile land in the region. It narrows to the north in the mountainous regions of Galilee and to the south in the desert regions of the Negev. It was a diverse but economically poor area with a mix of populations and no great river. To its west was a straight coast along the Mediterranean Sea that was not good for creating ports and made it susceptible to invasion. Despite being extremely fertile, the land also had frequent droughts, which meant the people were often in fear of a shortage of water and food. But the Fertile Crescent was the ultimate bridge, so everyone desired it and passed through it, and it was essentially the center of the ancient world.

God promises this land to the descendants of Abraham, not only as a blessing to them but also as a blessing to the world. Jesus echoes this sentiment in his Sermon on the Mount when he proclaims, "Blessed are the peacemakers, for they will be called children of God"(Matthew 5:9). God's people, eventually named the children of Israel, were supposed to use the influence and power of this land to share the love of God with all who passed through it. They were supposed to embody his plan to restore *shalom*, complete wholeness, to the land through love. Israel was meant to be a blessing to the world by sharing the truth of God's plan of restoration with all who passed through.

A BLESSING TO THE WORLD

That God's people were to be a blessing to the world was still a directive during Jerusalem's Second Temple Period when Jesus walked with his disciples. The same plan that had been given to Israel in its infancy was still God's plan generations later. When Jesus gives his final directions to his disciples, he commissions them to continue the plan of peacemaking that had already been laid out for the children of Israel. The Great Commission (Matthew 28:18-20) is believed to have been given at Mount Arbel, which sits at the northern narrowing of the Fertile Crescent and overlooks the Sea of Galilee. Surrounding the Sea of Galilee is the most diverse population in the region. To the west was Galilee, which was populated mostly by Jews. To the north was Gaulinitis, which was about half Jewish and half Gentile. To the east was the Decapolis, where Pontius Pilate had his palace and most of the Romans who had occupied the region lived. The population was majority, if not all, Gentile. As the disciples looked out, they would have recognized this region as a microcosm of the nations.

The key to understanding the Great Commission is to recognize that the word *go* (Matthew 28:19) is not a command. A better translation is "as you go." The actual command in the verse is to "make disciples." What is it that Jesus is asking of his disciples as they stand 594 feet above sea level overlooking the most diverse region in their world? Basically, he says, "As you are going about your day, make disciples of all the nations because they are right here! The directive is the same as what I told your ancestors. I have brought the nations to you. Your job is to share the love of God with all who are here and embody my plan to restore the world through love." Jesus makes the same promise to the disciples that was made to the descendants of Abraham: Just be faithful to me in the place I have sent you, and I will be with you.

A modern example of this is the emergence of American sanctuary cities, such as Chicago. They have become centers for immigrants and refugees, many of whom are coming from countries where international missionaries haven't had access. Due to extreme hostility to the gospel message, there are entire countries missionaries have not been able to penetrate. For this reason, "diaspora missiology" has recently emerged to complement both international and urban missions. It is a missiological framework for understanding and participating in God's redemptive mission among people living outside their place of origin: "It takes into consideration the increased openness to the gospel which often results when peoples are displaced from their homeland."[2] It helps us to realize the value of God's people being placed in every corner of the earth and the importance of proximity. Paul proclaims that God "made all nations to inhabit the whole earth, and he allotted the times of their existence and the boundaries of the places where they would live, so that they would search for God and perhaps grope for him and find him—though indeed he is not far from each one of us" (Acts 17:26-27).

The plan has never changed. God has placed us and has promised to send the nations. Whether we live in a crammed inner city or sprawling suburb, a majestic rural farmland or an intimate small town, wherever God has placed us our job is to share the love of God with all who are there and embody the plan for restoration through love. We are often looking for the next big thing, the next great place, or the next great purpose, but Jesus is asking us to make disciples right where we are. God wants us to love people as we go about our daily activities. As you go to the grocery store— make disciples! As you go to the laundromat—make disciples! As you go to work, school, sports practices, family outings, reunions, and even to run errands—make disciples! "By this everyone will know that you are my disciples, if you have love for one another" (John 13:35). If you will faithfully love the place God has given you, whether permanent or temporary, you can trust that God will be with you there.

Besides the Great Commission, the other place in Scripture we see Jesus giving his disciples some final directives is in Acts 1:4-8. What I love about this passage is that the disciples are trying to figure out what is going to happen now that Jesus has been resurrected. They ask Jesus if he is going to overthrow the Roman government and restore the kingdom to Israel. I love that Jesus' reply is basically, "None of your business!" He tells them they don't get to know what God is doing, but he can tell them where they are going: "You will receive power when the Holy Spirit has come upon you; and you will be my witnesses in Jerusalem, in all Judea and Samaria, and to the ends of the earth" (Acts 1:8).

Jesus wants to be clear that the plan has not changed. The plan is still that the children of God be faithful to the place God has given them. They should be witnesses there and trust that God will be with them. What I love is that Jesus gets specific about where he needs his people to be and makes sure his disciples understand that there is no place he will not be represented. Jesus is careful to name these places in a specific geographical progression, so that the disciples would not be mistaken about where he was asking them to place themselves. Most of the disciples were from the rural northern region surrounding the Sea of Galilee. They were considered uncultured, uneducated, and would have been more comfortable fishing, visiting family, and enjoying the familiarity of the area. This is the place of comfort where they would have loved to be his witnesses as they went about their daily lives at home or with family.

Jesus begins by naming Jerusalem and Judea as the first places where they would be his witnesses. Jerusalem was the major metropolis of the region and the hotbed of political, religious, and economic corruption. It was not their city of origin and would have been a cross-cultural experience for the disciples coming from Galilee. While they were acquainted with this place because of their time with Jesus there and because it was the city that housed the temple, Jesus was calling them to be witnesses among the powerful and corrupt political and religious leaders of their day. Judea was the mountainous, southern desert region of the land in which Jerusalem was located. This is a reminder that while they were called to the city center it was not to be to the neglect of the surrounding community. There is a move outward from home to the places of power and all of the places affected by its decisions. So, contrary to popular belief, the call to be witnesses in Jerusalem is not a call to stay close to home where you're safe and where things are familiar. It's a call to be present in centers of power, commerce, and culture, and the places affected by those decisions. Through this call Jesus urges us not to forsake the powerful.

Then Jesus names Samaria! The disciples' faces probably immediately changed because no one goes through Samaria. Jewish society already had an established narrative about Samaria and its inhabitants. Samaria was a place to avoid at all costs, even if it took you out of your way. The Samaritans were a people group that emerged through the intermarriage of Jews and Gentiles and were looked down on by the Jews because they were not of pure Jewish heritage. Jews would often travel an extra day's journey across the river just to avoid setting foot on Samaritan soil. Jesus was asking the disciples to be witnesses in the last place on earth they wanted to go. In this sense we can define Samaria the same way we define exile! What does this mean for them? There is no place that Jesus will not be represented and absolutely no people that God has forsaken. Jesus recapitulates the hard truths of his Sermon on the Mount in this directive by encouraging his disciples to love their enemies and be witnesses to all who will listen. Through this call Jesus tells us not to forsake the marginalized and outcast.

Lastly, Jesus says that they will be his witnesses to the ends of the earth. These seem like such honorable and noble words spoken over this ragtag group of fisherman, zealots, and tax collectors. However, the call to the ends of the earth would not have felt noble to this group at all, but rather terrifying. Going to the ends of the earth for these disciples who have never gone beyond the shores of the Mediterranean Sea would seem not only impossible but also intimidating because it would mean crossing what seemed to them to be an endless body of water.

Throughout the Old Testament we hear about troubled waters and dreaded sea monsters, such as Leviathan. A big fish even swallows Jonah. When Jesus is on the boat with his disciples and a storm comes that begins to beat against it, the disciples are afraid they are going to perish.

When Jesus says you will be my witnesses to the ends of the earth, the disciples would immediately believe that this was beyond their capabilities. This was Jesus' point all along. Through this call Jesus says you will be my witnesses beyond what you are capable. He was going to push them to be what they thought they could never be. When Paul comes along and begins to take Jesus' message across the sea, the disciples saw that Jesus' words were true. While Paul's missionary journeys are impressive, Peter and the twelve never strayed from the original command to make disciples as they go. They remained witnesses in their place rather than traveling to make disciples. But due to the diversity of Galilee, they too were being witnesses to the ends of the earth. By crossing into Samaria they were making disciples in places they would have never gone before and loving people they had never considered. When we are pushed beyond our capabilities and are taken out of our comfort zones, like the disciples on the boat, we too call on Jesus. Thankfully, he has promised to always be with us wherever we are and to empower us with the Spirit. Each of us has a place to which we are called, and we cannot be Jesus' witnesses without a deep concern for that place.

PLACE IS OUR IDENTITY

Throughout the Bible we see that people are often identified by their places. It is common for biblical characters to be referred to by their names and their places of origin: children of Israel, Jesus of Nazareth, Saul of Tarsus. The angels even address the disciples as "men of Galilee" in Acts 1:11. In modern American society, most people are disconnected and transient, identified by a myriad of characteristics (class, age, race, gender, etc.) but rarely by the places we live. I refer to this as "living above place." When Jeremiah speaks to the exiles, he encourages them to marry and have sons and daughters and to increase there and not decrease. He desires for their families to become invested in Babylon. Living out Jeremiah 29 means that generationally you become more rooted in a community. Your family name and values become more embedded in that community. Whenever I introduce myself to someone, one of the first things I say is that I live on the South Side of Chicago in the Englewood neighborhood. For me this is simply because I am unable to share my story without making my place central. It is a matter of discipleship. I love the place too much. I don't just want to be known as Jonathan Brooks. I am Jonathan Brooks of Englewood.

From the Old Testament to the New Testament we see that the identity of God's people is attached to where they are from or where they are going. Place is valued by God, and connection to Christ does not mean disconnection from place. We are told to root ourselves in a place and encouraged to be witnesses for God there. To prepare ourselves to be witnesses, we must know the history, demographics, assets, and needs of the places God sends us. Jesus expects us to do the work of learning and loving our places so that we can best witness to his love there. Jesus himself lived as an example of what we are asked to do.

In John 4 we find the well-known story of the woman at the well. This story has often been used, especially in Christian community development circles, to discuss empowerment and the recognition that everyone has capacity. This is a positive and appropriate use of the story. But I would like to focus on the events that led up to this encounter, to speak to valuing places that have been forsaken.

Prior to the interaction with the woman, Jesus and his disciples are fleeing from Judea back north to Galilee. The religious leaders had gotten wind of the fact that Jesus was making and baptizing more disciples than John the Baptist. They were already after John and would soon imprison and kill him for his actions. John has identified Jesus as the Messiah and the Son of God, and now Jesus needs to head back home for a little while to retreat from all the opposition. The difference between this journey and the many journeys the disciples had taken with him before is that this time Jesus says specifically that he has to go through Samaria. I am sure the disciples were not pleased with this because, as mentioned earlier, it was common knowledge that Jews and Samaritans had no interaction. The disciples would not have been excited about Jesus' sudden detour from the traditional route. Nonetheless they agreed, although probably reluctantly, to travel through Samaria on their journey from Judea to Galilee. After all, it was a quicker route.

When Jesus got to Sychar, near a sacred plot of ground that Jacob had given to his son Joseph, he sent his disciples off to go grocery shopping and he sat down by Jacob's well. It was noon, the hottest part of the day, and he was thirsty but had no way to get water out of the well. While he was sitting there a Samaritan woman came to draw water out of the well. This was strange. If you were going to carry heavy buckets of water, would you come at the hottest time of the day? Obviously, she was hoping not to run into anyone at the well. Jesus saw her and asked if she would give him a drink of water. Her response was interesting and one of the main points I want to make about the interaction. She looked at him and asked, "How is it that you, a Jew, ask a drink of me, a woman of Samaria?" (John 4:9).

As a Samaritan and a woman, she expected him, I'm sure, to respond harshly or even ignore her question. But Jesus goes on to offer a deeper relationship and challenges all her assumptions about the proper relationship between Jews and Samaritans. She focuses on the historic divisions between the two people groups: "Our ancestors worshipped on this mountain, but you say the place where people must worship is in Jerusalem" (John 4:20). But Jesus focuses on their unity in God: "The hour is coming, and is now here, when the true worshippers will worship the Father in spirit and truth, for the Father seeks such as these to worship him" (John 4:23).

Obviously, this initial interaction was not meant to be a lesson to his disciples, because they were off grocery shopping. When they return, they are astonished that Jesus is talking to a Samaritan woman, but they don't ask any questions. I believe this interaction is the real reason Jesus needed to go through Samaria. He needed to perform another miracle: challenging the Samaritan woman's prescribed stigma so that she could see herself as fully created in God's image. This miracle could not be done unless Jesus was physically in her geographic location. While there are many miracles Jesus is able to do by just speaking or praying for them, this miracle, the woman seeing herself as a full image bearer, only happened with his physical presence in her forsaken place. Jesus knows that the consequence of a stigmatized narrative is that the inhabitants of the place begin to internalize the lies about themselves and the places they live.

THE DANGER OF A SINGLE STORY

In 2009, African novelist Chimamanda Ngozi Adichie gave a riveting TED Talk titled "The Danger of a Single Story." She tells the story of how she found her authentic cultural voice and warns that if we hear only a single story about another person or country, we risk a critical misunderstanding.[3] In the Englewood community, residents are bombarded with negative images and media headlines. Rarely are images of our beautiful gardens or classic architecture disseminated. Far more often what is shown are abandoned buildings and trash-lined streets with broken glass. This leads residents to believe their community is not worth keeping clean. Nearly every headline in the news media highlighting our community is a report of violence. For many years this caused the neighborhood to own that narrative.

In 2012, King Louie, a Chicago-based rapper, coined the term *Chi-raq*. Around that time it was being reported that more people were murdered in Chicago than in the war-torn Middle East. While this was a citywide epidemic, the Englewood community and other neglected neighborhoods became synonymous with the term. In 2015, African American director Spike Lee chose Englewood as the community to film his satirical musical drama named "Chi-Raq," despite the community's split reaction to the singular connection of our community to this moniker. The film was about the girlfriend of a Chicago gang leader who persuades other women to abstain from sex until their men agree to end the senseless cycle of violence.

About a decade ago Oprah Winfrey did an exposé showing the differences in Illinois high school resources.[4] She did a school swap between Chicago's Harper High School in Englewood and suburban Neuqua Valley High School in Naperville. The students saw the dramatic difference in their schools, which are funded through property taxes, and were amazed. When the Harper students walked into the computer lab of Neuqua Valley, they couldn't believe their eyes. One student responded, "If this was our computer lab, the keyboards would be missing letters and there would be no roller ball in the mouse." A narrative that told them they did not deserve the resources that the Neuqua Valley students received was shaping the Harper students. Unknowingly, they were stating their belief that their fellow students might not appreciate or take care of the type of equipment they saw in the suburban school. One student remarked, "If we can't get it, I'm glad someone can."

Combating a seemingly informed, internalized lie is far more difficult than changing an ignorant, externalized one. When residents of a place begin to believe the lies or half-truths said about them, they begin to pass them down generationally. Then the lack of care and sometimes disdain for their place in turn becomes a disdain for the people who inhabit that place, including themselves. Jesus decided that he must go through Samaria to confront the prescribed stigma that had been internalized by the Samaritans. This affirming interaction where Jesus challenges the woman's beliefs about her self-worth begins a chain reaction. The Samaritan people began to have hope and desire to experience what the woman had experienced.

Communities all over the world experience this same internalization of labels placed on them by outside people and societal narratives and stereotypes. The perpetuation of one-sided narratives causes people to devalue the places where they reside, as well as the residents who live there. In my South-Side community, the hardest work we do is freeing the residents from the damage caused by the incomplete narratives they are constantly bombarded with through media images and artistic expressions, as well as real-life experiences. When people ask me how I propose we slow down gun violence in our communities, I often remark that it begins with reestablishing the value of place in our communities. When you don't value your community and can only see it as a place to avoid rather than to help flourish, you eventually begin to adopt the same value system for the residents of that community. If this place doesn't matter and you live in this place, then you don't matter either. It is much easier for me to take your possessions, your freedom, or even your life if I am convinced that neither my life nor yours matters.

Reestablishing the value of place is bigger than gentrifying communities and making them economically viable. It is about affirming

REMEMBER THE POOR AND MARGINALIZED

THE CHURCH-FORSAKEN PEOPLE

But seek the welfare of the city where
I have sent you into exile.

JEREMIAH 29:7

Honesty in my pen, integrity in my heart, this
ain't a big role, I'm just playing my part.

C. W. ALLEN

You want unity? Then read a eulogy. Kill the
power that exists up under you and over me.

LECRAE

CHAPTER SEVEN

NO MORE OUTREACH

We packed up our cars and closed the church after a successful Thanksgiving outreach where we gave away dozens of bags of clothing and nearly fifty turkeys. On the Tuesday before Thanksgiving for nearly a decade we have held this outreach for our community. This year's event had been bigger than ever as we provided frozen turkeys, free clothing, and a dinner we purchased, prepared, and served for the community. I was proud of the work we had done, and the congregation, although tired, was excited about how things had turned out. We were even talking about how we wanted to make next year's event even bigger and serve even more people!

As some of us walked to our cars and others toward our homes, a couple of people walked up and offered to sell us a couple of turkeys. On closer inspection we realized that these were two of the turkeys we had just given away less than an hour ago. Those feelings of pride and excitement we felt just minutes earlier as we were cleaning the church quickly turned to bitterness and resentment. One of our members commented on how ungrateful those people were and that they could have at least waited until we were gone.

Others made statements like, "This is why I don't waste my time helping people, because they just don't care about anyone but themselves." It was amazing to see how quickly our attitudes changed when the recipients of our compassionate giving did not respond the way we expected. We went from planning to make next year even bigger to being ready to cancel the event and never help these ungrateful people again.

But in the back of my mind I was thinking how smart it was for our neighbors to sell the turkeys. It was 100 percent profit, and almost all the congregation members were on their way to buy turkeys for their Thanksgiving dinners anyway. The problem was that while we had an abundance of turkeys at the church, our attitude was that we should not be recipients of handouts because we were the givers, not the receivers. After all, we know it is more blessed to give than to receive. I just couldn't shake the idea that there was more to this situation then we understood. Just as in the unfortunate event on Mothers' Day a few years earlier, I wondered if there was something we needed to learn from our neighborhood from this experience.

What exactly caused us to alter our view and see our neighbors as "those people who only care about themselves"? What was going on in us that made us so quickly want to cancel an event that we had sponsored for nearly a decade? Just minutes earlier we were excited about growing it even bigger than before. I thought about the words we used to describe our neighbors and began to realize how dangerous the dichotomy between community and congregation had become. We were the service providers and our neighbors were the service recipients. This had become the primary way in which we interacted with our neighborhood. When we did not receive the gratitude we expected, we were unable to understand our relationship to the community. We began to question our purpose for existing. We ceased to know how to exist as a church when we were not the provider or if the recipients were not satisfied with what we offered. In our minds, they should have been grateful for whatever we provided.

SEEKING SHALOM

Jeremiah moves towards the climax of this portion of his letter when he begins to challenge the exiles to see not only Babylon the place as valuable but also all that comes with it. They are told to seek the welfare of the place God has sent them. This means they have to understand the Babylonian social structures, backgrounds, languages, identities, and political climate. They must learn to value the customs and ways of Babylon. No longer should they be content with being outsiders who don't understand the culture. They are to become neighbors who seek the peace and prosperity of the Babylonians as much as their own families. This peace and prosperity that Jeremiah commands Israel to seek is *shalom*—a total human flourishing that results in the common good. It is living a communal life the way God intends, actively pursuing the best for everyone, even those you may not choose to be your neighbors.

This must have been difficult for exiled Israel to hear because they had lived with such an elitist attitude for generations. They did not seek the peace and prosperity of other lands and considered themselves better than all the surrounding tribes and nations. They were God's chosen people and therefore deserved respect, honor, and dignity. They did not mind helping others, but there should be no confusion that they needed no help from anyone else. Until now. After being conquered and exiled, this misplaced notion of self-sufficiency and national supremacy had taken a severe blow. This was never the way God intended Israel or any nation to live.

God's people were supposed to be living interdependently and sharing the love of God and his plan of shalom with the world. How is that possible when you have set yourselves up to be better than everyone around you? Jeremiah reminds Israel of their interdependence and challenges them to see what God is trying to accomplish by carrying them into exile. Until we are stripped of our ability to look down on others and until we truly find ourselves in need, we can never understand community. He urges them to seek the peace and prosperity of the very people they would have nothing to do with prior to God carrying them to Babylon.

REMOVING OUTREACH, EMBRACING COMMUNITY

Our small congregation is mostly made up of individuals and families who are just making ends meet themselves. When they decide to give of their time, finances, and talents, it is a real sacrifice. Therefore, it really mattered when it was not received well. No one wants to sacrifice only to feel unappreciated. Whether one gives sacrificially or out of abundance, everyone wants to feel appreciated for what they give. It is just human nature. The problem with the way we had been interacting with our community was bigger than feeling unappreciated. I watch my congregants consistently provide for their family and friends, knowing it is a thankless job. This issue was bigger. Everyone desires appreciation, but what we need, whether giver or recipient, is affirmation—to feel as if we matter regardless of the position we find ourselves in. Everyone needs to feel that they are contributing to the flourishing of the community. We needed to answer a core question: When the interaction is done, how can both parties leave feeling affirmed in their dignity and ability to contribute to community flourishing?

So I sat down with the leadership team and we began to process what we thought of our neighbors. Once we named these feelings, we assessed to see if this was the way we were operating as a congregation. Did we really believe we were loving our neighbors by providing for them but not seeing them as equal? What about us as a congregation? Many of us were struggling financially, so what made us only providers and never recipients? We began to realize that the idea of outreach was creating an us-versus-them mentality, which was contrary to our desire to be community oriented. We made a couple of decisions that day which we still hold on to tightly today.

First, we have completely removed the word *outreach* from our vocabulary and replaced it with the language of *community*. We still have our event but now it is our Thanksgiving Community Dinner. Any event Canaan sponsors or partners with will only use the language of community. This helps our congregation and community to remove the dichotomy and hierarchy. Churches are quick to use language like "the lost" or "unchurched" when planning events, but this focuses on what divides us. I am not sure what makes us think this is the most loving way to engage our neighbors. Canaan has decided to use language that describes what our congregation and community have in common. We learned that language matters when you are seeking total human flourishing for the common good.

Second, we recognize that we are both providers and recipients of love as members of our community. So, during our Thanksgiving Community Dinner, which anyone can help provide and prepare for, we no longer only serve but sit at the tables with our neighbors to eat, laugh, share recipes, learn each other's stories, and catch up. Our clothing giveaway is now a one-dollar discount store where our whole community shops together. Everything that can fit in a plastic shopping bag and can be tied closed is yours. (I promise you have never seen such creative packing or people tie tinier knots as we close up our bags!) It is one of my favorite times of the year because it is a beautiful picture of our community members taking care of ourselves. We have women's, men's, and children's clothing, dishes, bikes, shoes, jewelry, coats, and just about anything else you can imagine. It is truly a community effort.

Lastly, rather than giving away turkeys, we now have a raffle for three Thanksgiving baskets to which everyone donates and is eligible to win. Every member of our community is eligible, including members of the church. We no longer believe that because the event is held in our space that we are the service providers. We are all a part of this community, and we all have the opportunity to have our needs met. While the winners can do whatever they like with their prizes, we have seen raffle winners decide to bless other families. Others take them home because they were wondering how they were going to provide for their families this year.

Local churches are waking up to the damage that can be caused by our desire to be service providers and never recipients. Recent books like *Toxic Charity* by Bob Lupton and *When Helping Hurts* by Brian Fikkert and Steve Corbett, have helped to reevaluate the typical service paradigm. For Canaan, removing the language of outreach has led to a better understanding of true community. We now know community begins with seeing every person as someone with capacity and realizing we all have things to provide and things we need to receive. When we begin by seeing the gifts and talents of everyone in our community, we then have tangible means through which to meet each other's needs and desires.

THE POWER OF WITH

Being able to meet each other's needs using the gifts and talents of the community begins with a new understanding of what it means to be *with* one another. There is one main theological truth that separates Christianity from other religious beliefs. It is the belief that God is with us. The greatest promise we have in all of Scripture is this promise that God will be with us. In the Old Testament narrative God promises to be with Israel as they travel through the wilderness, to be with the judges and kings as they rule over the people, and to be with the prophets as they share difficult truth. In the New Testament, Mary and Joseph are told that their baby's name will be Emmanuel, which means "God is with us" (Matthew 1:23).

Jesus promises his disciples that as they fulfill the Great Commission, he would be with them even until the end of the age (Matthew 28:20). When he ascends to the heavens, Jesus sends us the Holy Spirit as a comfort and companion as well as a fulfillment of the promise that God will always be with us. In Revelation, as things come to a conclusion, we hear a voice yell from the throne: "Look! Look! God has moved into the neighborhood, making his home with men and women! They're his people, he's their God" (Revelation 21:3-5 *The Message*). Over and over again we are told that God desires and promises to be with us. There is a special power in knowing and remembering this truth.

In his 2003 smash hit "Jesus Walks," Chicago rap artist and super producer Kanye West made strong claims that upset some Christians:

> To the hustlers, killers, murderers, drug dealers, even the strippers
> (Jesus walks for them)
> To the victims of welfare for we living in hell here hell yeah
> (Jesus walks for them)[1]

While many were upset by the lyrics because they thought they lowered God's standard of righteousness, what I love about them is that they are an attempt to encourage those who have been traditionally left out of church and society. When he states, "Jesus walks for them," these lyrics insist that this song was not written for those who have it all together but for those who are still struggling and find themselves on the margins. We have to listen carefully to the stories of those around us to begin to understand why they are making certain choices. We do not get to decide who God is presently walking with or how the transformation process works for them. If we dismiss people because of their current choices without considering their stories, we put ourselves in a position reserved only for God.

We have used the phrase "the power of with" as an ongoing theme for Canaan. I simply began by asking the congregation to work on changing our language. For an entire year I challenged us to use no personal pronouns. We were changing our language from "I" and "me" to "us" and "we." Our music ministry switched the singular language in our worship songs to make it plural, our preachers used communal language in their sermons, and I even asked our first impressions ministers to greet people with plural language. If a visitor walked in they would hear, "We welcome you all to Canaan Community Church." I'm sure they got a few strange looks from visitors as they looked around to see who else was entering with them.

This language change also affected how we described what we were doing at our church and who we wanted to be. It made a drastic difference. Rather than saying that we wanted to serve our community, we began to say we wanted to serve *with* our community. Instead of loving our neighbors, we wanted to love *with* our neighbors. Instead of advocating for the oppressed, we wanted to advocate *with* the oppressed. Just a simple language change was beginning to change our practices as well. We made sure we did not create events, programs, or initiatives without including in the planning and implementation those who would benefit from them. We truly became a community church as we watched our community embrace leadership opportunities in partnership with the church. Our invisible lines of separation, which had been so prevalent in our ministry, were being destroyed by the power of with.

I NEED YOU TO SURVIVE

Willie stumbled into Sunday morning worship, barely able to stand and clearly out of sorts. When he came in the door, Deacon Mark, who happened to be standing in the back, grabbed him by his waist, put his arm over his shoulder, and walked him to a couple of seats that were set up in the back of the sanctuary. They both took a seat and Mark seemed to be trying to get Willie to look him in the eye. From my place in front of the congregation, I saw Willie lower his head into his hands and begin to weep. I was clearly disturbed by the scene, but Mark motioned to me to stay put. He looked at me as if to say everything was fine and that I should continue with worship. Throughout the worship service I watched Mark continue to console and comfort Willie. Mark never left his side and made sure he felt loved and cared for despite his impairment.

To close out worship, our congregation began to sing the gospel song "I Need You to Survive," by Pastor Hezekiah Walker. This is a song we sing quite often as a reminder of our belief in community as a kingdom value since it reminds us of our need for one another.

We then began to sing the words of the second verse, when we boldly declare that we will pray for one another and that we love each other. And something amazing, almost magical, happened. Willie reached out his hand to Deacon Mark, who grabbed it quickly. Mark helped to pull him up out of his chair and Willie lifted his hands in the air. Although he was unable to stay on his feet very long, for a few glorious seconds I saw the ultimate picture of the kingdom of God: Mark physically holding Willie up as he attempted to worship God while still dealing with the effects of drugs and alcohol.

In that moment I realized something that has stuck with me. Remembering the poor and marginalized does not mean helping people out once they have met our standards of righteousness. It means including them in the redemptive work of worship, repentance, and reconciliation *even in the midst of* their struggles.

Not only was that moment transformative for Willie but for Mark as well, as they both sang out the final verse:

You are important to me
And I need you to survive.[2]

It would be nearly impossible to sing those words while literally holding up your brother who is unable to stand on his own and not be changed.

If we are truly going to be a new kind of church, a church that remembers the marginalized and outcast in our community, we have to become more concerned with loving people than lording policies. We must spend our time focusing on those things that unite rather than those things that divide. Willie, although clearly impaired, was freely included in our worship on that Sunday and is still included in our congregation to this day. Since then he has brought his wife, Geraldine, who also struggles with drug addiction and other health-related issues. We have welcomed her to be a part of the Canaan family as well.

While we know that there is spiritual wickedness happening all around, we at Canaan know that addiction is a health issue and not just a sin issue. Therefore, although we know that they still struggle with their addictions, they are completely included in our church family. We look for them when we have not seen them in a while. We constantly remind them that we are here for them and want them to seek professional help for their issues. However, we do not ostracize or alienate them for choosing to do otherwise. While we do not condone the damage that they are doing to themselves and their loved ones, we recognize that the work of inner transformation is beyond our control. God is the only one who can change a heart, and we believe that God is very good at this job. We must focus on our responsibility. If God changes the heart, what are we called to do as their church family?

LOVE EVERYONE

Jesus is clear that the responsibility of the church is to love. Multiple times in the Gospels Jesus tells us that our primary responsibility is to love everyone: "Let me give you a new command: Love one another. In the same way I loved you, you love one another. This is how everyone will recognize that you are my disciples—when they see the love you have for each other" (John 13:34-35 *The Message*). In the Sermon on the Mount he says, "You're familiar with the old written law, 'Love your friend,' and its unwritten companion, 'Hate your enemy.' I'm challenging that. I'm telling you to love your enemies. Let them bring out the best in you, not the worst" (Matthew 5:43-44 *The Message*).

Jesus' followers are clearly expected to love one other. However, Jesus pushes us even further and challenges us to love our enemies as well. Since Jesus is telling us to love our friends and family as well as our enemies, it seems obvious that we should love everyone in between as well. Jesus confirms this when he encourages the Pharisee to answer his own question about how to inherit eternal life. After the religious leader answers correctly, "You shall love the Lord your God with all your heart, and with all your soul, and with all your strength, and with all your mind; and your neighbor as yourself," Jesus, responds, "You have given the right answer; do this, and you will live." But the religious leader, wanting to justify himself, then asks, "And who is my neighbor?" (Luke 10:27-29). Jesus responds by sharing the story of the Good Samaritan.

Jesus not only puts a Samaritan, whom the Jewish religious leader would have never seen as a neighbor, in the story, but he makes him the hero. Then he takes two characters, a rabbi and a priest, whom the religious leaders would have easily seen as neighbors, and has them miss the opportunity to be neighbors. He closes the story by asking who was a better neighbor to the man. This question is so important because it focuses on the responsibilities of those who say they follow Jesus. We are to be far more concerned with loving people than worried about whether they agree with us or even fit our narrow notions of righteousness. The Samaritan saw the man, knew he was Jewish, and knew that he would probably not help him if the shoe were on the other foot. Still, he sacrificed and included him in his life.

Loving everyone does not mean excusing damaging behavior, poor attitudes, rude stereotyping, or injustice of any kind. As a matter of fact, love is a tangible action that resists and reforms all those things. In order to truly love one another we must have difficult conversations and name the ways we hurt others and ourselves. We also must not look for reasons to separate ourselves from one another but for ways to unite around those things we have in common. Traditionally, the church has been focused on detailing and expressing those things which separate and divide us. This is why I believe the church needs to become more compassionate and learn to love unconditionally while still standing for righteousness. We must be able to see people who have been traditionally forsaken by the church and value them for who they are, not who we think they should be. All people are created in the image and likeness of God, no matter how marred, so we must desire to include as many as possible. The more kinds of people we include, even those we don't understand or struggle to agree with, the more complete our understanding of God becomes. Understanding people's stories gives us access to parts of God that we may not have seen without their presence.

Willie and Geraldine have opened the eyes of our congregation to a fuller image of God—a God whose grace is always sufficient in their struggle even if their addiction, like Paul's thorn, is never fully removed. It has been quite a journey walking with them down this difficult road. However, there have been times when Willie and Geraldine have in turn held me up when I was struggling with life's difficulties. On their good days, as they call them, Willie and Geraldine will sometimes stop by the church or sit with me on my porch. Before they leave, they always ask to pray for me. Our journey together is not over and is always a reminder that God's grace will be sufficient for us all as we seek wholeness. We know that God specializes in changing hearts, so we want to specialize in loving unconditionally.

THE FORSAKEN CULTURE OF HIP-HOP

Not only has the church forsaken individuals but often entire cultures. One culture that the church has done a poor job of connecting with is hip-hop. Even in this age of multiculturalism and ethnically diverse worship practices, hip-hop music and culture are still considered a novelty. I will admit that I am a bit biased and maybe there are other cultural representations that have been equally misrepresented. However, I can say unequivocally that there is no culture in the world that has a broader reach than the hip-hop culture.

This culture that began as a rebellious cry from the streets of the Bronx in New York has become a global phenomenon. It has influenced every area of popular culture such as music, dance, language, fashion, and much more. In a time when the Bronx was being heavily neglected not only by the society but by the church as well, this culture was created to bring peace, love, and unity to a community that had been filled with hopelessness. The culture was all about taking lemons and making lemonade. With little investment in music programs or musical instruments, the creative disc jockeys began to take their parents' records and use the breakdown of the popular disco music of the time to loop two records and create their own music to dance and perform over. Buildings were dilapidated and were being burned daily, but the graffiti writers used their spray cans to create murals in order to beautify their own communities. Breakdancing was created as an alternative to gangs and fighting. If you had a problem with another breakdance crew you did not fistfight, you battled it out on the dance floor. The emcee had the opportunity to not only energize the party but poetically narrate the true conditions of these neglected neighborhoods. These are the roots of this culture. It is important for the church to realize that the three tenets of hip-hop—peace, love, and unity—are very much in line with our Christian beliefs.

I have traveled internationally and domestically to both large urban centers and remote rural villages, and the impact of hip-hop reaches them all. I remember being in the rural villages of the Massai in Kenya, standing inside a tiny wooden hut with a tin roof and seeing spray painted on the ceiling "Nelly iz here," an homage to the St. Louis–born rapper Nelly. When I traveled to Nairobi to visit pastors living and doing Christian community development in Kibera, the largest slum in the world, I heard the sound of the latest hip-hop blasting from barbershops and corner hangouts. It does not matter where I travel—Asia, Europe, Africa, North or South America—the reach of hip-hop is dramatic and sustainable everywhere. I can always find amazing graffiti murals, a club with hip-hop as its main attraction, as well as those whose fashion is clearly impacted by this culture. The ethos of the culture has been passed on for generations and doesn't look to be going away anytime soon.

What worries me about the church's relationship to hip-hop is that we still consider it a novelty that appeals to youth or young adults. The church just uses it as an attention getter. There was even a push to speak of hip-hop culture as a tool used to reach young people for the purpose of bringing them into the Christian faith. Allow me to make a comparison in order to prove how problematic this approach is. A family of Indian ethnic descent visits a local congregation. The next Sunday the church sings songs infused with traditional Indian sounds and serves the cultural foods of India. Regardless of their ethnicity, everyone dresses in traditional Indian garb as a tool to win them to Christ. We recognize this to be problematic and patronizing because we know that culture is not a separate tool for manipulating individuals; it is a core part of their human identity. We would never want to offend them or make them feel as if we do not value the beautiful culture they bring into our congregation. However, repeatedly I am asked to come to local congregations for their hip-hop services or events to get the young people's attention so that the message of Christ can be shared. Pastors will "dress down" for this event and try to use language they otherwise would never use to "reach" the young people in their congregation or community.

While hip-hop still speaks to youth culture in an overwhelming way, it is now over forty years old. There are pioneers in the culture who are well into their sixties and consider this the culture with which they most identify. It is frustrating and condescending for this global culture to still be considered something specifically for youth and young adults, when many hip-hoppers are now middle-aged adults. Churches that have not recognized the importance of this culture will find themselves not only struggling to relate to youth and young adults but to the middle-aged adults in their congregations and communities as well.

In 2015 I had the opportunity to lead worship for the Christian Community Development Association conference in Memphis, Tennessee. One of the first requests I made was to have a DJ on the stage with me as part of the band during the worship set. Too often DJs are used as novelty acts before things get started, but then the worship leader will naively say, "Now everyone, it's time to worship," as if the DJ were not just worshiping God using the turntables. My friend Pastor Terence Gadsden, aka DJ Rock On, was an integral part of the worship sets that year and we were able to infuse elements of hip-hop into the worship experience seamlessly. While I am sure some were uncomfortable or surprised by this infusion, many others shared with me how encouraged they were to see hip-hop represented from the main stage during worship. It helped them to worship in the way that spoke most clearly to them.

Having someone who loves God and hip-hop culture as the worship leader that week was the reason that the elements authentically spoke to the hearts of the hip-hop worshipers in the audience. I did not have to manufacture anything; there was no language to learn or cadences to memorize. I was able to be authentically who God designed me to be, and because of that, this culture, which has long been forsaken by the church, was able to be received by its representatives in its purest form. People of all ages, ethnicities, genders, and communities were positively affected and for the first time felt included.

WHEN HIP-HOP GROWS UP

One critique of hip-hop culture that comes from within is that it has not matured with its people. In his song "Peter Pan," hip-hop artist Sho Baraka eloquently lays out the issues with hip-hop culture not growing or speaking to the daily issues of those who have matured into the next phases of life (marriage, parenthood, career, etc.). The song closes with these lines:

> They need extended adolescence so they can blow up.
> Hip-hop you're close to fifty, when can we grow up?[3]

A young couple I counseled and whose wedding I officiated helped me to see the influence of hip-hop as it is maturing. During their final counseling session, we talked about their finances and they amazed me with a decision they had made. They told me that while some of their friends were easily spending twenty-five thousand dollars on weddings, they had decided to scale back on their wedding because they wanted to invest in a friend's business venture. They took ten percent of what they were going to spend on their wedding and invested in their friend's small business startup. I asked them what prompted this decision? They talked about listening to "Family Feud," on Jay-Z's 4:44 album and hearing him ask:

What's better than one billionaire? Two

'Specially if they're from the same hue as you[4]

"That statement made so much sense to us," they continued. "Why should we spend our money making others wealthy when we could be investing in our friends and peers?" I knew in that moment that hip-hop culture had moved to another plateau.

Soon after that conversation another young person asked me how much it would cost to buy a piece of Hebru Brantley's artwork. Brantley is a Chicago artist majorly influenced by the South Side's AfriCOBRA (African Commune of Bad Relevant Artists) movement in the 1960s and 70s. He created the iconic characters Flyboy and Lil Mama. His artwork has been collected by Chicago Mayor Rahm Emanuel, the Pritzker Family, and power couple Beyoncé and Jay-Z. My response to her was simple: "As big as Brantley is, you will need to put thousands away."

She responded quickly, seemingly unrattled, "I think I'm going to do that."

I couldn't help but ask, "Why do you want to buy a Hebru Brantley piece? Are you a fan of his work?"

She responded, "Yes, I am, but I also heard Jay-Z say he bought some artwork for one million, and two years later it was worth two million, so I figured it must be a pretty safe investment."

In everyday conversation young people are quoting hip-hop artists as motivation for their financial decisions. Many of these young adults are first-generation middle income. They came from poor parents but find themselves in college or trade school or starting businesses. Our congregation has created a culture of going to school and even provides a scholarship in the name of one our first deacons, Edward T. Dunn. We also push young people toward entrepreneurship and financial freedom if they desire. When they come back from school or are moving toward middle- to upper-class lifestyles, they are trying to figure out how to get to the next level.

This is such a reminder of the power of hip-hop culture. Though in the past it may have guided people to make poor decisions about their finances and health, it is having a much more positive influence as it matures. Hip-hop culture is growing up, learning more, and seeing more. Therefore, the generation that's coming up behind me will experience it in a different way. We have to be careful about how we frame the popular music we hear on the radio. What is an artist actually saying underneath their lyrics? We have to listen with a different kind of ear. When an artist boasts about material possessions like big houses, fancy cars, and expensive clothing, we must not dismiss it as only superficial. They are also narrating the feelings of those who have traditionally been forsaken by society once they lift themselves and their families out of poverty. For a real hip-hop listener, it is important to hear where an artist begins and critique how they evolve. Hip-hop has helped me have conversations with my neighbors and parishioners about economic empowerment and the holistic human flourishing that God desires for us. So while they are thinking about how they are passing down a financial legacy, I like to ask what legacy they're passing down spiritually, mentally, and physically.

The documentary *Feel Rich: Health Is the New Wealth,* directed by Peter Spirer, explores the emerging self-love revolution. It contains interviews with people who have made great changes in their lives by redefining what it means to be rich.[5] These are hip-hop icons as well as others influenced by hip-hop culture talking about holistic flourishing. Some of them are vegans and some have opened their own juicing bars. They explain how although they had money and fame they still were not happy. You can get as much money as you want, but if you're not healthy enough to enjoy it, it does not matter. This includes the need for spiritual health.

NO ONE LEFT OUT

Jeremiah writes to the exiles in Babylon exhorting them to seek the peace and prosperity of everyone in exile. No one is to be left on the outskirts. They were to seek shalom for the entire community, including those they may not know as much about or understand. For Israel this means that they must not only affirm individual people but the Babylonians as a people group and culture. As they increase in number there and seek Babylon's long-term welfare, this transforms the Babylonians into family. Israel must now learn what aspects of Babylonian culture are acceptable to God as they seek its prosperity.

Similarly, the church must see hip-hop as a part of the family. For many it is a way of life that is being passed down generationally. Learning to love hip-hop culture will not come from study or training; it will be picked up through proximity and presence. Being present in hip-hop spaces, attempting to worship through hip-hop music, and seeking to understand the God-honoring aspects of hip-hop culture are ways of engaging. Even as a pastor I find myself in hip-hop spaces where God is not being directly honored by the music or atmosphere. However, I often feel more welcome there than many church services and events. I am not alone in this.

I had the chance to go to Jay-Z's *4:44* tour and Lecrae's *All Things Work Together* tour on consecutive nights in Chicago. I traveled to both concerts with a group of pastors and church leaders also heavily impacted by hip-hop culture. We spent both nights discussing how much we value the moments where we can be our authentic selves and not feel like outsiders. Even after writing books, pastoring churches, and working in neglected neighborhoods for decades, we still feel as though most churches misunderstand our culture. For example, some people contacted me surprised by my presence at the Jay-Z concert. For them it does not make sense for Christians to support this music, but for us it is a way to honor the music and culture that made us who we are. We often listened to these artists and cultural pioneers more than politicians, preachers, and sometimes even our parents. Both concerts were impactful moments of community in different ways. The Jay-Z concert was an opportunity to connect with fellow hip-hoppers and celebrate the beauty of the culture. The Lecrae concert was an opportunity to connect with fellow Christians and celebrate Jesus through the beauty of hip-hop culture. Both concerts and sets of concert attendees were important to God. No one was forsaken. It felt like everyone at both concerts wanted the same things: love, peace, and unity. Including God.

CHAPTER EIGHT

AIN'T A THAT GOOD NEWS?

While I was a student at Tuskegee University, my love for the diversity of hip-hop music grew dramatically. Along with my favorite artists, I had now been exposed to a whole new world of hip-hop artists who loved Jesus and were not ashamed to proclaim it. They were just as zealous to talk about Jesus as artists like Wu-Tang Clan were to talk about the five-percent nation.[1] One of the things I love most about hip-hop is its ability to lift up marginalized voices. In college I sang with the Tuskegee University Golden Voices concert choir, which specialized in Negro spirituals. As we studied the music to sing for chapel services, God began to open my ears to the powerful sound and resilient messages of these spirituals, also referred to as "code songs." They were sung by enslaved Africans while working in the fields and were not only songs of resilience but of hope, as they often carried secret messages signaling escape routes to the North for freedom and liberation.

One of my favorites that we sang was the spiritual "Ain't a That Good News," arranged by the Tuskegee choir's first conductor, Mr. William Dawson, also known as the dean of Negro composers.

The lyrics tell of the oppressed people of God recognizing that all that they have been deprived of in this present time is readily available to them in the kingdom of God. Now, while the writers of the song originally equated the kingdom of God with a future place and time, the message is still relevant for those of us who believe the kingdom of God is not only a future reality but also a very present one.

> I got a crown up in a de kingdom
> Ain't a that good news
> I got a crown up in a de kingdom
> Ain't a that good news
> I'm a gonna lay down this world
> Gonna shoulder up a my cross
> Gonna take it home a to my Jesus
> Ain't a that good news

The song goes on to speak of having a harp, a robe, and a savior in the kingdom. This premise can be problematic if you believe that kingdom is only a distant, otherworldly place. But if you believe that Jesus has ushered in the kingdom of God with his incarnation, these words can be both comforting and informative for the church's responsibility to present-day society. Jesus said, "The time is fulfilled, and the kingdom of God has come near; repent, and believe in the good news" (Mark 1:15). When Jesus came, the kingdom of God was inaugurated. All that we sing about that will be fully realized in the kingdom to come are realities we pray and work for today. Another negro spiritual that speaks to this idea is "Walk All over God's Heaven."

> I got shoes, you got shoes
> All of God's children got shoes
> When I get to heaven gonna put on my shoes
> Gonna walk all over God's heaven, heaven
> Everybody talking about heaven, heaven
> We're gonna walk all over God's heaven.[2]

Similar to the previous song, this spiritual speaks of the future realization of a present need for the enslaved people singing the song. We may be working the fields now, and the oppressive overseer may not give us shoes, but when we get to heaven we will have shoes because God cares about us. While this is a message of future hope, it does little for their present shoeless situation. This is why songs like these were also code songs for escaping to the North, where these enslaved people felt they would find liberation, freedom, and yes, even shoes, here on earth. Ultimately, the songwriters knew that the gospel of Christ had to be good news for everyone and every situation or it was not the gospel at all. Good news to the poor and oppressed is not just the message that they will be free someday, but that God sees them now and is already working on their behalf. This is why Jesus began his ministry by going to the temple, unrolling the sacred scroll of Isaiah, and reading these words:

> God's Spirit is on me;
>   he's chosen me to preach the Message of good news to the poor,
> Sent me to announce pardon to prisoners and
>   recovery of sight to the blind,
> To set the burdened and battered free,
>   to announce, "This is God's year to act!" (Luke 4:18 *The Message*)

The good news of the gospel is God's promise to act on our behalf. Jesus wanted the world to know that God was already working on behalf of the poor, imprisoned, blind, burdened, and battered. Imagine if the church could remember that this is to whom we are called to share good news. This kind of good news follows God's lead and announces, "This is the church's year to act!" Ain't a that good news?

REMEMBER THE POOR

The church has a clear responsibility to society, which is summed up beautifully in a small but powerful early church interaction described in Galatians 2:8-10. The early church leaders only gave Paul and Barnabas one command as they were starting their missionary journeys to the Gentile nations. Although the early church had differences of opinion about how the good news was to be shared and to whom, there was one thing that was unanimously agreed on regardless of where in the world ministry led them: the church must remember those on the margins of society.

I argue that Matthias was the disciples' choice to replace Judas. Unfortunately, they were not patient enough for Jesus to make his own choice. Casting lots was a socially acceptable way of making decisions and was used as a way seeking God's guidance. But really, who advised Peter to draw straws? What about Jesus' ministry led them to believe that it was his desire that they choose a replacement? While Matthias joined the ranks of the apostles at the beginning of the book of Acts, ultimately, Jesus chose Saul while he was riding on the road to Damascus.

I don't know why Jesus chose him, but based on his resume, I can think of a few reasons why Saul was a good choice to be the voice to the Gentile nations. He had tremendous academic and religious acumen, a passion for truth and a willingness to go to great lengths to champion that truth, and ready access to travel between Jewish and Gentile places because of his dual citizenship. When Paul and Barnabas were about to leave on their missionary journey, they went before the leaders of the church to receive their blessing. Prior to this Peter and Paul had already disagreed as to whether the message of Jesus was meant for the Jews or the Gentiles. Although the two disciples never agree on the correct plan of action, they agree to support each other and their specific directions from Jesus.

The biblical narrative goes on to tell us that while praying for Paul and Barnabas and commissioning them on their journey, Peter challenges them to agree to only one request before they leave—to remember the poor as they travel. Paul, not to be outdone by Peter, responds by saying that they were already eager to do that (Galatians 2:10). I can see Paul's face turning up and him mumbling under his breath, "Peter is always trying to make me look bad. I know that remembering the poor is essential to following Jesus."

I believe this is still the one request that Jesus is making to the church. Those who consider themselves his followers have a responsibility to remember the poor in their daily activities. Wherever we travel, whatever our responsibilities, interwoven into our very being is the command to be thinking about the most disenfranchised in our society. No matter our specialty or passion for ministry, every church should be eager to remember the poor, marginalized, and outcasts, for this is what it means to be the church.

REMEMBER YOUR PRIVILEGE

Beyond the need to remember those on the outskirts of society is another valuable lesson we gain from this exchange. Paul had a passion for truth and a willingness to go to great lengths to champion that truth. He also carried the most privilege of all the disciples because of his academic and religious training and his dual citizenship. This interaction between Paul and Peter gives us a glimpse into how to use privilege for the advancement of the kingdom. Something to consider is that Jesus may have even chosen Paul because he was a person of privilege. His life can be an example of what it looks like to lay down privilege for the sake of the kingdom. Everywhere he goes, because he is an educated male with economic resources, he can walk right into the synagogue. He has no fear of speaking his mind because of the assurance and protection of his citizenship.

Very few disciples had the freedom and confidence to travel back and forth across the sea or the ability to sustain themselves financially in the manner of the apostle Paul. With this cultural understanding, this conversation becomes bigger than two apostles disagreeing over conflicting methodology. It becomes an in-depth discussion about the existence and use of privilege. Peter is reminding Paul that his connection to Jesus is a connection with those on the margins of society. He encourages him to stay connected to the poor as he travels freely through spaces of privilege and power. The purpose of his trip is not just to speak truth to the rich and powerful. He must stay connected to the people who will remind him why he was going to these powerful spaces in the first place.

Many of us have been awakened to the places where we carry privilege, such as gender, race, class, and identity. Our congregation, through connecting with other ministries and churches in Africa, has realized that even at our poorest, we are financially privileged. For this reason, I push our congregation to support ministries abroad, even as many of us struggle to take care of our own families. The Englewood community also recognizes this. When the Flint water crisis happened in 2016, although the median income level in our community was well below the poverty line, a group of community residents, organizations, and churches purchased water, shampoo, soap, and other basic essentials, loaded up a truck, and delivered it to the students and staff of a local elementary school in Flint. We have a responsibility to use whatever privilege we have for the furthering of the kingdom of God. Peter and Paul's interaction shows us how important it is to connect to those society has marginalized so that we can recognize how and remember why we are to use our privilege.

Tim Dearborn, former director of the Lloyd John Ogilvie Institute of Preaching at Fuller Seminary, often speaks of an actual physical *re-membering* of the parts of the body of Christ that we have tried to discard. He uses this language to say that if we disconnect from one another, we are like a body walking around with missing limbs. This imagery is a beautiful reminder of our need for everyone in our society to be valued, heard, and affirmed. Paul says it best:

> The way God designed our bodies is a model for understanding our lives together as a church: every part dependent on every other part, the parts we mention and the parts we don't, the parts we see and the parts we don't. If one part hurts, every other part is involved in the hurt, and in the healing. If one part flourishes, every other part enters into the exuberance. (1 Corinthians 12:25-26 *The Message*)

Remembering the poor is a command of Jesus that helps us relinquish power and privilege. We are called to focus on the growth of the kingdom of God versus our own personal prosperity: "But strive first for the kingdom of God and his righteousness, and all these things will be given to you as well" (Matthew 6:33). This is what Jeremiah wanted Israel to understand and what I hope to help each of us to understand. If we seek the peace and prosperity of the people and places we have typically tried to avoid, there is a special blessing and lesson in it for all of us. We must begin to see those on the margins of society. When we do we will find ourselves closer to one another, closer to our purpose, and closer to Christ.

NOT BAD BUT BLIND

Nowhere in the biblical narrative does Jesus articulate the movement toward the marginalized and outcast more clearly than in the parable of the sheep and goats in Matthew 25. This passage is an in-your-face reminder that our actions toward those on the margins of society are a direct reflection of our connection to Jesus. Once again, when it comes to our relationship with the poor, we want to answer the action questions of what, who, when, and why but don't want to discuss where. The problem is not that we don't know what to do, it's that there are certain people and places we don't see. In his sermon "Love in Action," Dr. King said, "They know not what they do, said Jesus. Blindness was their trouble; enlightenment was their need. . . . The men who cried crucify him were not bad men but rather blind men."[3] Jesus confirms this when he states the reasons why some people will be goats and some will be sheep. The problem is not ill intention but the inability to see those around us and thus to act on their behalf. From this passage I suggest three "looks" we need to take to see one another better and to see Jesus in our everyday interactions.

First, Jesus tells us to take a look *for the lowly*. All too often we look for Jesus in the wrong places. Jesus' preferred place of residence is with the outcast and marginalized. Even as the high and lifted-up Lord, he prefers to be among the most disenfranchised. This parable begins with Jesus as the judge on the throne dividing up the people of the world into two groups: those who are his and those who are not. This seat is the epitome of power and authority, so Jesus makes sure to establish this place first. However, by the end of the parable those he is judging are asking him when they saw him hungry or thirsty, naked or in prison? His response is that what they have done to the least of his people they have done for him. What is Jesus saying? When we look for Jesus, there is a specific group of people he likes to spend his time with—those whom most people ignore. So if we want to know where to find him, then we must pay attention to those that we would typically ignore or push to the side. When we ignore them, we are ignoring Jesus. When we pass them by, we are passing Jesus by. When we are too busy to attend to their humanity, we are too busy for Jesus. Jesus tells us to look toward the lowly because most of us are not bad people; most of us are just blind.

Second, Jesus tells us to take a look *beyond limitations*. In the parable the goats are perplexed because they do not remember ignoring Jesus. They were most likely taking care of their families, tending to their occupations, praying daily at the temple, and doing other religious activities. Maybe they just felt like the world's problems were too big for them to tackle. Jesus explains that it is easy to become distracted by our own lives and our limitations and miss opportunities to experience God in new ways. In this parable the sheep are not better people than the goats. They simply took time to think of others in the midst of their busy lives. Both groups seem surprised that their treatment of the most marginalized in society is what separates them from the other group. Neither seems to have known that Jesus was present amongst the hungry, thirsty, naked, or imprisoned. So what is it that separates them? What makes one group sheep and the other goats? It is the activity of the sheep and their ability to see past their own limitations and trust the provision of God. When you give of your food to someone who is hungry, you must trust that you will have enough food left over after giving. When you give a drink, you must believe there will not be a drought for which you needed to store up water. Giving up your time to visit the prisoner might mean that a meeting will have to be shifted or that "me" time may have to be rescheduled for the week.

We all have limitations and worry if there will be enough time, enough money, enough energy, enough of everything. Jesus is not challenging us to sacrifice for others out of fear that he might be testing us, but rather so that we can learn to trust God enough to go beyond our limitations. When we begin to see the people that society has tried to forget, as big as their needs may be, we realize that giving our treasure and time to one another is how God designed us to live. This is not only about material possessions, although we know from this passage that God desires us to have food, drink, clothing, housing, and caring relationships. The ability to receive reciprocal affirmation of our humanity and the blessing of understanding someone else's life experience leads us towards mutual transformation. If we want to see Jesus, we have to be willing to look beyond our limitations, for it is when we are just beyond our limitations that we step into a true dependence on God and one another.

Finally, Jesus challenges us to take a look *for less*. What first comes to mind when we hear the word *less* is our material possessions. While I am a proponent of simplicity as a Christian value, I'm not talking about not owning a television or only buying secondhand clothes. I am speaking of letting go of the desire for some superspiritual enlightenment whenever we lean into the uncomfortable aspects of Jesus' message. There is often an underlying belief that when we sacrifice for our faith there will be some significant spiritual experience on the other end. However, even the eyes of the righteous have trouble seeing Jesus amidst the busyness and chaos of life.

As mentioned above, the righteous are just as surprised by Jesus' response to them, which causes them to ask when they saw Jesus hungry, thirsty, naked, homeless, or in prison, just the same as the unrighteous do. This means that the righteous did not engage in any of these activities expecting any special recognition or because they expected some spiritual enlightenment to happen. When they fed the hungry, they did not post it on social media and receive hundreds of likes. When they gave drink to the thirsty, they did not call the news media to report the event. There was no special reward for taking in the homeless or visiting the prisoner. It seems that the righteous engaged in these activities just because they were the right things to do. Their love for their neighbor was not contingent on the neighbor's response or their own emotions.

So when Jesus tells them that he saw their work and was present among those they took time to love, they are surprised. Their intention was not to receive accolades from God but to genuinely care for their fellow humans. To look for less means to remain diligent and affirm the humanity of all people simply because it is the right thing to do. We are not to expect special feelings or highly emotional spiritual moments as a result of loving neighbors, although that could happen. We are also not to expect special accolades or awards. We are simply to remember those marginalized by our society and our churches, hoping to one day regain their trust and enter into relationships of mutuality with them. Sometimes the best that will happen is that we will love a stranger well for a moment and then walk away with nothing more than the remembrance of that moment. Jesus challenges us to look for less, to see the human interaction as a priceless gift more valuable than any spiritual or emotional experience we may expect or try to create.

THE GREAT EQUALIZER

There is a church in our neighborhood called Chicago City Life Center, located at 5501 South LaSalle. The pastor is Charles Moodie, a young African American who moved to Chicago from New York City. Whenever you ask Pastor Moodie about his congregation, he will tell you that he pastors the unusual suspects—people churches typically push away because they are dealing with drugs, alcohol, homelessness, prostitution, and other issues. He will often say that any Sunday you enter their gymnasium, which doubles as their sanctuary, it will reek of alcohol. However, what Charles understands is that the gospel of Jesus Christ is the great equalizer. It is a message of hope and healing for those who traditionally have been on the outskirts of society.

Canaan is partnering with City Life Center and other Englewood churches during our One Englewood One Church unity campaign. Whenever our churches have evangelism events or prayer walks or get together to fellowship, it is the amazing members of City Life

Center that are most present and eager. These "unusual suspects" are ready to work the hardest and are the most dedicated because they know from where God has brought them. Jesus chose the unusual suspects as his leaders as well. They were a ragtag bunch of leaders who were not considered the elite of their day. These kinds of leaders have nothing to lose because they have already experienced rejection and marginalization. They are totally reliant on God, day in and day out.

In Luke 3, John the Baptist is introduced as the forerunner of Jesus who is proclaiming a baptism of repentance for the forgiveness of sins. The words used to describe his message echo a prophecy from the book of Isaiah. This prophecy is one of the most powerful proclamations of what happens when the people repent of their selfish ways and desires. It explains that John's purpose was to proclaim the coming of Jesus the Messiah whose ultimate purpose was to reveal God and reconcile all people to him.

> Thunder in the desert!
> "Prepare for God's arrival!
> Make the road straight and smooth,
> a highway fit for our God.
> Fill in the valleys,
> level off the hills,
> Smooth out the ruts,
> clear out the rocks.
> Then GOD's bright glory will shine
> and everyone will see it.
> Yes. Just as GOD has said." (Isaiah 40:3-5 *The Message*)

In the original prophetic passage we get a glimpse of the prophet proclaiming the entrance of the presence of God. The proclamation signals a clear path for God to go before the people and details the lengths they are to go to ensure a smooth arrival. We see the ground being leveled off, any debris on the path being cleared, and the roads being made straight and smooth. The hills and mountains are excavated and all the soil and rocks are dumped into the valleys in order to make sure the ground is level. The prophet then goes on to say that once the road is properly prepared, the bright glory of God will shine and everyone will see it. It is not until the high places are brought down and the low places are brought up so that the road is even that the glory of God is able to shine.

When we translate this equalizing language back into the context of the book of Luke, we see John speaking to the religious crowds of his day. He warns them not to think of themselves more highly than they ought by lifting themselves up as Abraham's ancestors or followers of the law. He encourages them to realize that repentance, a change of desire and behavior, is necessary to receive forgiveness of sins. By echoing the proclamation of the prophet, John makes sure that all who hear him recognize that they are on the same footing when it comes to their need for this Messiah. It did not matter what their ancestors had done or how long they had been following God. They had forgotten what their position in Egypt felt like and were enjoying being lifted up like mountains. John reminds them that all who have been lifted high will be made low, and all who have been low will be lifted up.

This message of bringing the high down and the low up is echoed throughout Christ's ministry. It is one of the main ways Jesus emphasizes God's love for all. John is proclaiming the most important sentiment of the good news that whether our life circumstances have lifted us too high or made us feel low, we all need Jesus. That is basic truth of the message: we all need Jesus. When there is anything else we feel we need more than him, we are missing the truth and are unable to see or follow him. John says when all the other issues are removed, then and only then will our crooked ways be made straight and our rough places made smooth so that

God has a clear path to our lives. There is absolutely no person that God has forsaken. At the end of the day all of us have the same need for a Savior who loves us more than we understand.

THE UPSIDE-DOWN GOSPEL

Some interactions Jesus has during his ministry provide examples of this equalizing message. The first interaction is a conversation between Jesus and a young, wealthy man looking for answers. He asks Jesus what seems a simple question: "What good deed must I do to have eternal life?" (Matthew 19:16). However, it seems Jesus does not want to answer the question because the young man is looking for a simple action or good deed he can do that will appease God and secure his eternal comfort. Jesus begins by asking the young man why he came to him. There is only one who is good, Jesus says, so obey the commandments of God.

Interestingly, the young man is confident that he has obeyed all the commandments of God and is wondering what else he could do to make sure that he and God were on good terms. This is where the story gets interesting. Jesus is not fooled by his arrogant show of righteousness, but he does not challenge his answer at all. When the young man asks what else he can do, Jesus immediately begins the process of exposing what he held dear to his heart. Rather than responding that the young man should just believe in him, Jesus encourages him to sell everything he has, give the money to the poor, and then follow him. Jesus needs to make sure the young man realizes that the road to eternal life begins with a total reliance on him. Here we see someone who has traditionally been lifted high that needs to be brought down to the level of total dependence on Jesus. If there is anything else we depend on more than Jesus, that's what needs to be removed so that we can see him.

In the second interaction, recorded in Luke 8:40-56, Jesus is fresh off his encounter with the man he had healed of the legion of demons. Jesus is now walking in a crowd of people with his disciples. Jairus, a leader of the synagogue, asks him to come to his house and heal his only daughter who is dying. While on their way the crowds of people surrounding Jesus are getting out of control. Everyone is pressing in tightly, trying to get close to him. A woman who had been hemorrhaging uncontrollably for twelve years makes up her mind that if she could just touch the very tip of his robe she would be healed. She presses through the crowd even though she was considered ceremonially unclean and should not have been near anyone. She comes up behind Jesus, reaches her hand through the legs of the people in front, and snags the very edge of his robe. She is immediately healed of her issue.

Jesus, although surrounded by people on every side, stops the crowd and asks who touched him. Peter glances at Jesus with a look of confusion and says, "Really Jesus? Everybody is touching you. Look at this crowd!" Jesus replies, "You don't understand. Some power has left me; this was a different kind of touch" (Luke 8:45-46, my paraphrase). The woman realizes she can't hide any longer and she jumps up and tells him what she did. Jesus' response to her is simple: "Your faith has made you well" (Luke 8:48). There was no extra she needed to do. He didn't tell her to follow him or give up anything. Her faith was more than enough. It was simply her realization that she needed him that made her whole. Here is an example of someone who traditionally had been made low and it was her total dependence on Jesus that made her whole and lifted her up.

There are many other examples of Jesus rebuking, challenging, and humbling the rich, powerful, and well respected throughout his ministry, such as the parable of Lazarus and the rich man, the parable of the rich fool, and Jesus' encounter with Zacchaeus the tax collector. Those who have been lifted high need to be brought down in order to realize that their greatest need is a total reliance on God. There are also many interactions where those who find themselves marginalized by society because of gender, ability, economic status, marital status, incarceration, and immigration status are lifted up because of their total reliance on God, such as the woman caught in adultery, the blind man by the pool of Bethesda, Mary and Martha after the death of Lazarus, and the Samaritan leper who came back to thank Jesus. Those who come to Jesus as their only hope are affirmed because of their faith.

Jesus is urging the church to proclaim this upside-down gospel. If we are going to re-member the poor and marginalized in our communities, there is an affirming message we need to be sharing with them. Churches have traditionally done a poor job of this because we preach as though everyone is coming from the same starting point. When people have been lifted high by society, local churches often make special accommodations for them, such as roped off seating and special entrances. However, Jesus urges us to challenge them so that they recognize their total dependence on God. Those who have been marginalized often come knowing Jesus is their only hope. They need to be lifted up for their total reliance on God. As Isaiah proclaims boldly, when the mountains are brought down and the valleys are lifted, all people will be able to see God. So we must be prepared to preach the message people need to hear, whether that's to sell everything and follow Jesus or to know that their faith has made them whole. Either way the end goal of this upside-down gospel is for everyone—rich or poor, powerful or weak—to recognize their total dependence on God.

Jeremiah wants Israel to seek the total flourishing of their exilic home, where no person or people group is left behind or left out regardless of their place in society. Remembering the poor and marginalized is part of seeking true shalom. No person need ever feel unimportant or left out of God's plan of redemption, reconciliation, and transformation. The beauty of the gospel message is that it is good news for all who hear it, both in this life and the life to come. Like Israel, we are not just given the task of seeking the peace and shalom of our place, but we are given a message to share that resonates with all who will hear it. Ain't a that good news?

PRACTICE SIX

REMIND ONE ANOTHER OF OUR COLLECTIVE POWER

THE CHURCH-FORSAKEN PURPOSE

Pray to the Lord on its behalf, for in its welfare you will find your welfare.

JEREMIAH 29:7

The church is the only organization that exists solely for the benefit of its non-members.

ARCHBISHOP WILLIAM TEMPLE

Go to the people. Live with them. Learn from them. Love them. Start with what they know. Build with what they have. But of the best leaders, when the work is done, the task accomplished, the people will say "We have done this ourselves."

ATTRIBUTED TO LAO TZU

CHAPTER NINE

SHUT DOWN THE CHURCHES

One of my family's favorite games to play as we drive down Ashland Avenue on the South Side of Chicago is called "Church Signs." First, we try to count how many churches we see as we drive down this main artery in our city. While the numbers don't come out the same every time we play, one time we counted upwards of ninety church buildings between 55th and 95th Street. Second, we try to find the most unique church signs and names. If you are familiar with African American church culture, you'll know that we are never disappointed because there are definitely some interesting ones.

Ashland is one of the few streets that stretches from the north to the south side of the city. Churches of all kinds line it: tall stone and brick cathedrals with beautiful steeples and pristinely kept stained glass windows, warehouses and garages turned sanctuaries, as well as dozens of storefront properties initially built for commercial use but converted for use by small congregations. Many of these storefront churches not only occupy space on the same block but literally share walls with one another. The storefront church phenomenon in Chicago is nothing new; it has been a part of the church culture here for decades. There are an estimated 390 churches in the greater Englewood community according to a report from the Chicago Police Department Seventh District headquarters. Canaan has a one square-mile target area in which we focus our community efforts from 51st to 59th Street (going north to south) and from Ashland to Damen Avenue (going east to west). In this one square mile there are approximately twenty-five churches.

When churches purchase buildings that were earmarked for commercial enterprises, it heavily affects the economic well-being of the community. When a congregation moves into that space, due to their not-for-profit status they pay no property tax and are exempt from city water bills. This means that hundreds of buildings designed to not only meet community needs but to pour back into the economic fabric of the community are no longer economically viable. Even if a congregation garners individual wealth, its exemptions mean it has the choice to reinvest in the community. On top of that, if the congregants live outside the community—maybe even outside the city—then all their individual property taxes and revenue are also directed outside the community. If the church is in no way connected to the hopes, dreams, and desires of the neighborhood, or at least praying for community flourishing, it is merely a drain on resources. All this is to say that I don't believe we need more congregations in our community; what we need is a strong presence of the church.

This problem is not limited to inner-city Chicago. As I travel I see this phenomenon just as clearly in rural and suburban spaces. Large, sprawling church campuses are located across the street from bustling shopping centers that have little to no connection to the marginalized in their communities. Some have gymnasiums, swimming pools, exercise rooms—facilities which the local schools may not even have—and ten-thousand-seat sanctuaries. I have met rural congregations who because of distance only use the physical building once a week yet are still struggling to stay connected to the needs of their towns throughout the week. Dare I say that in many neglected neighborhoods all over the country people are overchurched but underrepresented. There is no shortage of congregations or church buildings, but there are few truly community-focused ministries.

TRUE PROSPERITY

As Jeremiah comes to the close of this part of his letter, his focus switches from tangible physical presence to spiritual care of the place of exile. He urges the people to pray on behalf of Babylon and all its inhabitants. Alongside the holistic, tangible work of loving their neighbors, the people of God were expected to pray for the total flourishing of the community. It was not enough just to be present physically; their spiritual presence and total reliance on God was key to the process. Jeremiah goes on to say that their own prosperity is wrapped up in the prosperity of Babylon. Israel had to connect their spiritual power with the cultural understanding and leadership capabilities of the Babylonians. They had to realize that unless they partnered with their neighbors and prayed for God to lead them, they would never experience true prosperity. But what will this prosperity look like?

In Isaiah 65 the prophet describes an eschatological vision of a prosperous city—a futuristic utopian city as God designed it to be. In this city joy is overflowing and pain and anguish are no more. Long life is expected and secure quality housing is available for everyone. There will be nourishing food that all have had a hand in growing, harvesting, and sharing. People will be fulfilled by meaningful work in careers that use their gifts and passions, and they will work for the betterment of society, not just for a paycheck. There is no more killing, whether animal or human. Whatever we need from God will already be available before we even ask.

A similar eschatological vision was given to John during his exile on the island of Patmos. In Revelation 21 God's city is called the New Jerusalem, and its description echoes some of the same features as the city described by Isaiah. He also says there will be no more crying, no more dying, no more sorrow, and no more pain in this city. He also describes this holy city extensively with actual dimensions and amazing detail. Giving the city's dimensions—about 1400 square miles—helps us see that many diverse people living in relatively close proximity is a kingdom value. We also know this because John reaffirms what Isaiah said about the people dwelling in the city with God forever.

True prosperity is care for one another through proximity and presence, resulting in safety, health, vocation, longevity, strong family structures, and most importantly, the presence of God dwelling with us. This seems impossible to us, but Jeremiah encourages Israel to pray. The only way this true prosperity can be achieved is through partnership. While both visions were future prophecies, they reveal the heart of God and show us what true prosperity looks like. Until this becomes the norm in the places God has sent us, we must work together for the flourishing of our communities. We, the people of God, are the initiators of this work because God has called us to seek the shalom and pray on behalf of our communities. This praying for and seeking shalom may take us to the people and places we least expect.

AMEN TO TRANSFORMATION

After leaving a meeting where it had been announced that Chicago Public Schools (CPS) was closing fifty-one elementary schools because of underutilization, Asiaha Butler, who was the chair of the Community Action Council for Robeson High School, wrote a blog post that began with these words: "Since CPS is closing all of these schools for underutilization, some of these churches locked up with gates and chains all week need to be closed down for underutilization!"

I sat at my computer reading those words and began to think back on the many games of Church Signs my family and I had played while driving down Ashland. I thought of the formula CPS was using to decide whether a school building was being underutilized: at least thirty students per classroom. I thought to myself if that same ratio was used in churches, ninety percent would be shut down. As I sat thinking about a response to justify the church's behavior and building usage, I was at a loss for anything viable. I was the first to comment on her blog, but all I ended up writing was "Amen."

A few weeks later I saw that a new group called the Resident Association of Greater Englewood (RAGE) had been formed. These were young leaders in the community who wanted to galvanize and amplify the voices of the residents. They were asking for resident volunteers to help with the various civic, educational, geographical, and economic decisions being made for our community. I learned that Asiaha, who was called Mrs. Englewood, was a part of the team that helped to start the association. I decided to go the village meeting to hear what would be discussed and hopefully to meet this young woman who had spoken so prophetically to the church in Englewood. I hoped my presence and a brief conversation could offer a different perspective on the church. I attended the small gathering of residents held at the Kelly Library. I saw a few familiar faces that I had met in other spaces and gatherings in the community. I introduced myself as Jonathan Brooks, a resident of West Englewood who had been connected to this community my entire life. I conveniently left off my pastoral title.

After the meeting I was able to connect with other residents who wanted to see our community flourish. I repeatedly heard residents speak of Englewood returning to its identity as a working-class community rather than embracing the singular narrative of violence. I waited until most of the room cleared out and only a few leaders (in their red RAGE shirts) remained. I walked up to Asiaha and introduced myself, finally using my title: "My name is Jonathan, but everyone calls me Pastah J. I'm the one that responded 'Amen' to your blog about shutting down the churches." She seemed intrigued that I would respond that way as a pastor. We sat down for another hour discussing her feelings about the churches, as well as my hopes and dreams for Canaan and Englewood.

I left there determined to prove to her that there was another expression of the church in Englewood. I understood her sentiments but believed there was still hope for our local churches to wake up and see our responsibility to be a part of the fabric of the community. A few months later she asked if she could hold a meeting at Canaan, which would be the first time one of the resident association meetings was held in a church building. She had begun to see that clergy and the church could be viable partners in transformation.

REIMAGINING ENGLEWOOD

While I was outside the church playing football with some young people from our afterschool and summer program, the Diamond Academy, I was interrupted by an older woman standing on the corner of 55th and Paulina. She looked a little confused and asked if anyone knew the pastor of this church. I reluctantly raised my hand and began to walk over to where she was standing. She looked me up and down carefully and said, "Well, young man, it is wonderful to meet you."

I replied, "Likewise."

She said her name was Jean Carter-Hill and she had started an organization named "Imagine Englewood If . . ." in 1997 with the goal of creating social change and improvements in the quality of life for Englewood residents. She had lived in the community for nearly fifty years and had spent most of that time trying to make life better for residents. I immediately knew that this was someone I needed to know. I turned back to the young people and let them know they could keep playing but I needed to sit down and get to know Mrs. Carter-Hill.

In that impromptu meeting on the steps of Canaan I learned more about our community than I had in my twenty-plus years of living there. She talked about her fight to combat the issue of lead poisoning and her work with the Community Assisted Policing Strategies with the Seventh District police station. She told me about her organization's after-school and summer programs, as well as the number of young people she had helped find employment and achieve higher education. I was already amazed and enamored by her presence, but what she said next was the most profound thing I heard that warm summer afternoon. She looked at me and said, "Most of all, I am a woman of faith, but I don't understand why it is so difficult to get support from the pastors in the neighborhood. I was hoping that as a young pastor in the community, who works with lots of youth, you might be receptive to working with us."

Although saddened by the reality of what she said, I was reminded that this was the reality of our community. While there were many amazing people working to see our community flourish and combat the decades of neglect, the local church was often perceived as apathetic or reluctant. I made a decision on those stairs to make sure that the community knew the church was a viable partner in community transformation. I wanted them to know that there were some churches who would step up and intentionally ask how we could participate in community flourishing.

Through encouraging Israel to seek the peace and welfare of their exilic location, Jeremiah reminds them to slow down and pay attention. If I had not slowed down long enough to sit on those steps, I would have missed a wonderful partnership. No matter what kind of community you live or work in, I encourage you to seek out the elders like Jean Carter-Hill. Take Jeremiah's advice and pray. Specifically, pray for an elder who can give historical perspective and collaborate on issues in your neighborhood. Jean passed away recently, and her daughter asked me to speak on behalf of the pastors in Englewood at her homegoing celebration. It was an honor to hear her say that Jean always thought highly of me. I hope she knew the feeling was mutual. Today the organization is led by a young West Englewood native and Howard University graduate, Ms. Michelle Rashad, who is creatively continuing Jean's legacy of reimagining Englewood.

BECOMING THE RULE, NOT THE EXCEPTION

As time went on I became even more involved in what was going on in the community. I was partnering as much as possible, challenging our congregation to get involved with community organizations and the resident association and to get to know our neighbors. As we began inviting them to join in the work that was happening in the community, new people began to join our congregation. What was most encouraging was the people coming to be a part of our church were not leaving other churches to join ours. Most of them were coming because they did not have a local church body and were excited that they could walk a few blocks and find a congregation that cared about every area of their lives.

In 2010 we made the decision to cut our ties with the Missionary Baptist denomination and rename our church. This was not because we felt the denomination was evil, but our focus was our geographic community not our denominational affiliation. What we learned from many of our neighbors was that the denomination was sometimes a hindrance for people who identified with the specific beliefs of another denomination. When asked about their beliefs, many Christians will respond by naming a denomination before they say they're a follower of Jesus. Many African Americans have some historical connection with the church in their childhood. Many of us were taken to church by an elder in our family, and the denomination of that congregation can be extremely important to us. Our neighbors were saying things to me like, "I really love the work your church is doing, but I can't go there. I was raised Church of God in Christ, and my grandma would turn over in her grave if she knew I was going to a Baptist church!" I heard similar statements about other denominational affiliations as well. So we decided that we would remove that issue altogether by not associating with any one denomination and instead focus on truly becoming a community church. Being a community church means that we may not all share the same beliefs or ways of understanding worship, but we love our community. We want to see Englewood become all that God desires her to be. Therefore, we work through our differences to honor our collective goal.

I was invited to participate on a cable-access channel news show that RAGE was hosting. They asked me to talk about our church's work in Englewood and why we were concerned about the growth of the community rather than just our own congregational growth. That evening I shared with them much of what I am sharing with you in this book. The listeners from around the city seemed encouraged that there was a movement of people of faith who recognize that God is concerned with community transformation and not only individual transformation. After another show called "Real Talk with RAGE," the association composed a tweet that was taken from a comment made on the call-in hotline. The statement has stuck with me and has become a mantra for me as I continue to learn what it means to practice presence in neglected neighborhoods:

Tweet 🔍

R.A.G.E. Englewood
@Join_RAGE

The churches need to step up in Englewood and @PastahJ is the exception and should be the rule...#RealTalkWithRAGE cantv.org/hotline

6/16/16, 7:51 PM

The churches need to step up in Englewood and @PastahJ is the exception and should be the rule . . . #RealTalkWithRage cantv.org/hotline.[1]

My response was:

Although the inconvenient truth of this post is not missed on me. These are the moments of encouragement I need in order to keep working especially during difficult times. Much love to @Rage_Englewood and residents for showing @CanaanLoveGP & me some love and recognizing our love for this community. #ssslove #goodinenglewood[2]

GOOD IN ENGLEWOOD

You will notice I ended my response with a couple of hashtags. The first is #ssslove, which stands for Canaan's mission statement to "share, show and be shaped by love." However, the second, #goodinenglewood, is a phrase coined by Ms. Rashanah Baldwin, a young woman from Englewood. She has worked in journalism, community development, and other arenas and is known for her ability to help accentuate the positive characteristics of our community. She coined this phrase as a way of combating the negative narrative that was being disseminated about our community and to present a resident-led response highlighting the amazing things happening among the everyday people who reside here. I encourage you to take a minute to search this hashtag and scroll through the great work that has been chronicled and shared through this effort for years now.

Recently Rashanah wrote an article in a locally published magazine called *The West of the Ryan Current*, which highlights the communities to the west of the Dan Ryan Expressway. This highway is a major thoroughfare in our city that has often been used to separate poorer neighborhoods from more affluent ones. This expressway bordered many of our housing projects on the South Side and is used as a dividing line to keep certain communities insulated from others. Rashanah's article was titled "Why Black Church Should Matter to Black Millennials." She interviewed me and another local pastor about what our churches were doing to attract young people that was different from others in the community.

While the interview was a helpful opportunity to share about our congregation, for me the most rewarding part was seeing Rashanah's renewed trust in the church as a viable partner, as well as her own reconnection to a local church body. She wrote the article because her faith had been reenergized by the community reconnection of a local congregation, St. John AME Church, the oldest congregation in Englewood that was led by Pastor Kevin Andre Brooks at the time. It was encouraging to see her begin to connect her development and rebranding efforts to a local congregation and watch them come alive as a beacon of hope in the community. This is what happens when we reconnect to God's purpose for the church. The local church is not created for its own benefit but for the benefit of its community and residents. We are called, like Rashanah, to highlight and participate in the good work in our communities and to be present with and praying for our neighbors during the difficulties we all experience.

ENGLEWOOD RISING

All this narrative reframing and the work of RAGE has motivated a group of Englewood organizations and residents to begin our own full-scale rebranding campaign called Englewood Rising. This is a community-led marketing campaign that hopes to create positive change and highlight the rich history, culture, and value of the Greater Englewood neighborhood. The Englewood Rising website describes it this way:

We are embarking on a journey to engage residents by having our
community define the voice and essence of Englewood, instead of having
others define it for us: Our people, our culture, our progress, our neighborhood. Englewood has many strengths that often go unnoticed by
those outside of the community. This is our opportunity to show ourselves and everyone that our neighborhood is thriving once again.[3]

Canaan has once again offered herself as a resource for this rebranding campaign and participates as much as the community
residents see fit. There have been so many creative rebranding
initiatives that have come from this campaign, and it is an honor
to know that the residents recognize Canaan as a local church
contributing to the thriving of our community. However, I also
recognize that it's the decade plus that my family has lived in the
community, the relationships I have made, and the trust I have
built that has allowed Canaan to remain a name synonymous with
transformation in our neighborhood.

When we as residents decided to move forward with the rebranding campaign, we chose to fund it ourselves. We also advertised
it ourselves and made sure we—and not the media—owned the
complete narrative of our community. We purchased englewo-
odrising.com so that we could curate the stories of the residents
who live in our community. I was honored to represent Canaan as
one of the first residents profiled on the new website.

Next, we raised funds and purchased billboards in our
community. We gathered photos from many of the events sponsored by residents all year long, which became billboards displaying
everyday people enjoying their lives. We also included photos by
local photographer and artist Tonika Johnson from her exhibit
"Everyday Englewood," which captures the underrepresented beauty
in our Englewood community.

One of the photos displayed on the billboard was a picture of
my oldest daughter, Jasmine, hugging one of her teammates during

the inaugural season of the Englewood Police Youth Baseball League. This league was created to strengthen relationships between the Chicago Police Department and youth of the Englewood community through baseball. Police officers coached the teams and had the chance to build relationships with local youth. It was so exciting for my family to drive down Ashland Avenue, the same street where we play Church Signs, and see our daughter's face on a billboard with the caption: "There Is Love in Englewood."

This was a powerful experience for our family. Our daughter had been feeling frustrated by the way her neighborhood was perceived by outsiders, including some of her classmates. She wondered why people only talked about the negative aspects of our community and was beginning to get frustrated with constantly having to defend it. I will never forget her response when I drove her by so she could see the billboard. She looked at me and said, "Now everyone can see the same neighborhood we see." I was reminded in that moment of the power of positive images and realized these billboards were more than just a rebranding tool; they were an act of resistance to the constant barrage of negativity our residents endure.

A few months later I was awakened on my birthday by a text message from Asiaha Butler saying, "Look whose smiling face I see on 55th and Halsted." I opened the photo on my phone and it showed a billboard with my image on it and the caption "I Am Englewood." This was an amazing announcement to wake up to on my birthday and was a reminder that the community valued my work and the work of our congregation. I was humbled, but most of all I was proud of the genuine partnership that had formed. It was hard to believe that my face was on a billboard representing the very community I had tried to escape some twenty years earlier. While I was working to better the life of my community, the community was bettering my life as well. That realization hit me hard that morning. The Brooks family had connected to our place so well that we were being represented generationally in a way that brought honor to our community. The two billboards were proof that we were being identified by our place. We were not just the Brooks family; we were the Brooks of Englewood.

This moment was also a reminder of the genuine power of partnership and proved to me that true partnerships must be mutually beneficial. It is much easier to do for our neighbors in the form of outreach or benevolence. However, it takes far more energy, insight, discipline, and patience to listen to our neighbors and come alongside them as we collectively work for the betterment of our

community. Not only is this process slower—at least as far as typical success markers are concerned—but it is often more complicated because of the various thoughts, needs, and desires of the community. Ultimately, partnership takes longer, but it is worth it.

ONE NOTE AT A TIME

So many partnerships have been birthed out of this desire to come alongside our neighbors and have been mutually beneficial to our congregation and community. One of the most impactful has been our partnership with the Chicago Children's Choir, an organization that helped nurture me as I grew from a young boy to a teenager on the South Side. I belonged to this choir from 1989 to 1997 and had the opportunity to sing in just about every neighborhood in Chicago and all over the country, including the White House. I also had the privilege of traveling to Mexico, Japan, Russia, Poland, South Africa, Austria, and Italy—all before graduating from high school! Let's just say as a young man growing up on the South Side, this choir and the vocal training it provided gave me exposure I would have never otherwise received.

In 2013, Josephine Lee, the president and artistic director, announced that they would be starting an Englewood Neighborhood Choir. This, of course, was music to my ears, and I met with their director, Lonnie Norwood, to begin the process of partnering with them as they got this choir off the ground. Once they acquired rehearsal space, our church began recruiting young people in the community to join the choir. I offered my story as a testimony to the choir's impact on my life for families all over the community. For the first two years our church even partnered with the choir to sing Christmas carols for our neighbors. We called this event "Joy to the Wood" and it has grown significantly over the years. They now sing for many of the resident Christmas programs and even in the Englewood Square at the Whole Foods. However, it was

not until a friend and choir alum, Mrs. Sarah E. Dennis, EdD, began
to archive the history that I realized how significant the choir's past
was for my belief in the transforming power of the presence of the
local church.

The story of the founding of what became the Chicago Children's
Choir began in the fall of 1956, with about twenty-four young
children approximately eight to twelve years old, as the junior
choir of the First Unitarian Church of Hyde Park. Presently, the
Chicago Children's Choir includes over 4,800 children and teen-
agers, ages eight to eighteen, from every zip code in Chicago. They
sing in ten neighborhood choirs and eighty Chicago Public Schools
choirs. There is also DiMension for young male voices and Voice
of Chicago, the top performing and touring ensemble. Its founder,
the late Rev. Christopher Moore, was a visionary minister with a
commitment to social justice and music. He came to the First
Unitarian Church of Chicago in 1956 as an assistant minister while
he attended graduate school at the Meadville Lombard Theological
School. He was later appointed as minister of music to children
at the church.

Though I was aware of most of this history as a young singer
in the choir, it means so much more to me now as I work to
partner with my community as a local church pastor. It confirms
my belief that the work the church begins does not necessarily
have to continue to be led by the church in order to do the work
of God. The Chicago Children's Choir is no longer a faith-based
organization, but I am living proof that God is still working through
it. They are breaking down walls of division one note at a time by
exposing young people, many from neglected neighborhoods, to
people and places they may have never experienced. This work
began in a local church and is a reminder of the relevance of local
church bodies when they see themselves as a part of the collective
flourishing of neighborhoods.

There is power in partnership. When it happens, small dreams can become breathtaking realities. I am so thankful for the impact of this choir on my life, and I have countless friends, many who I consider adopted family members, who would say the same thing. We never know the impact our partnerships in the community will make. Reverend Christopher Moore and the First Unitarian Church did not know that their commitment to community partnership in 1956 would impact me so profoundly and become the catalyst for the work of Canaan Community Church today.

ENGLEWOOD PROSPERS, I PROSPER

I often reflect on my journey of returning to the South Side of Chicago, and it is remarkable how Jeremiah 29:7 has played out in my life. I began as a young man itching to leave Chicago, but it turned out that my future was bound up in the prosperity of my own city. When I moved my family into Englewood, I tried to protect them and make sure they felt safe in our new home. However, it was only when we got to know our neighbors and truly moved into the neighborhood that we ever really felt safe.

I was worried about whether my family would have healthy food to eat. But once we had to be concerned about what was available in our neighborhood, we became involved in the process of increasing the availability of healthy food options. Now my family is able to sip lattes in our own neighborhood coffee shop and purchase organic food from our own grocery store.

I stopped looking at the youth of our neighborhood as "those" children and recognized them as "our" children, wanting the same for them as I want for my daughters. Until then I never understood that it was my responsibility to walk through life with them in order to make an impact for generations to come. The kind of young women I want my daughters to become should be the kind of young people I want surrounding them. That does not happen by insulating and isolating them but by giving all children access to the same opportunities and care as my own.

This is why Jeremiah encourages the exiles to pray for Babylon and reminds them that in its welfare they would find their welfare. Every time I reflect on this truth or get the opportunity to speak about it, I am nearly brought to tears. This is a truth that I have not just read but have had the privilege to live for the last fifteen years. When Englewood prospers, I prosper. This is the God-given purpose that the church has forsaken—the importance of mutually beneficial relationships. When a local church's focus does not begin with the collective flourishing and mutual benefit of the surrounding neighborhood and its residents, then I would have to agree with Mrs. Englewood: It's best if you shut it down!

CHAPTER TEN

THE POWER OF PARTNERSHIP

A s our church's neighborhood food cooperative began to set up
our booth at the Englewood Arts Fair for the Whole Cities Foundation Grant competition, we realized just how powerful it was for
our church to be selected by community residents as one of the
nine finalists for this high-quality food access grant. Now we don't
spend much time chasing grants as a church. We realized a long
time ago that often the strenuous amount of reporting necessary
and outcomes stipulated can move us away from our original vision.
However, this one was different because it was resident chosen. We
were to present an idea for access to healthy food to our neighbors
who would then decide which groups would receive the grant.

Although we were the only church that participated in the process,
we were still selected as a finalist out of the dozens of organizations
and individuals who applied. The irony was not lost on me, as just
a few years earlier some of the same residents were asking for
churches to close their doors. Now they were willing to trust one
of us with community funds and believed the money would be used
for community flourishing. Though ultimately we were not chosen

to receive the grant, we learned a valuable lesson that conveys the power of partnership: Reputation matters.

REPUTATION MATTERS

Acts 2:42-47 describes how the disciples were all together, devoting themselves to teaching, fellowship, the breaking of bread, and prayer. Awe had come over everyone because of the amazing signs and wonders done by the apostles. They were together all the time. They had all things in common. They would even sell their possessions so that nobody had a need. Every day they spent time together in the temple, ate at each other's homes, and shared with generous hearts. However, there is a small part of Acts 2:47 that we often overlook, which speaks directly to the reputation of the early church: "Having the goodwill of all the people." Eugene Peterson paraphrases it this way: "People in general liked what they saw" (*The Message*). This is followed by the statement that day by day the Lord added to the number of those who were being saved.

While the verse does not directly indicate that the disciples were mindful of the flourishing of the entire community, it does show that the way the church operates in a community can garner goodwill from its neighbors. I believe that when we have a common concern for all people both inside and outside of the church, it allows others in the neighborhood to see that the church does not exist for its own benefit but for the benefit of all. This is true partnership and can lead to a new reputation where people come to see your local congregation in a different light. The Bible tells us that if we lift up the name of the Lord, people will be drawn to God. For many Christians this has been reduced to singing, praising, and preaching within the walls of our church buildings. However, I believe having a common concern for the everyday needs of all our neighbors should be added to the list of activities the church is doing daily. The first church showed us that reputation matters. Now we need to show that we can balance the needs of the church with a concern for the prosperity of the surrounding community.

LIVING AND LEARNING

A poem often attributed to Lao Tzu is well known in Christian community development circles and can be used as a road map for what it means to practice presence.

Go to the people;
Live among them;
Love them;
Learn from them;
Start from where they are;
Work with them;
Build on what they have.

But of the best leaders,
When the task is accomplished,
The work completed,
The people all remark:
"We have done it ourselves."

Notice the expectation is that you live with and learn from your neighbors before you claim to love them. I often introduce what I call the "Pastah J Remix" because the original quote implies that someone is moving into a community to lead people.

Return to or remain in our communities,
Live together,
Learn together,
Love one another,
Start with what we know,
Build on what we have.

I believe the true hope is for the people of the community to be empowered to remain in their communities and see transformation happen from the inside out. In chapter three, I introduced Mission

Year, a yearlong service learning program that allows young Christians ages eighteen to thirty the opportunity to live, serve, and grow in the city. I served as the Chicago city director for this organization. My main responsibility was to be the point person for the young people as they lived in the city as I mentored them, spent one-on-one time with them, and secured volunteer service sites for their year. But I also have had the privilege of partnering as a local pastor as well. I have had teams living in West Englewood and attending Canaan for the last two years.

What I have learned about partnership through Mission Year is the importance of living and learning. Many of the young adults who participate in the program know nothing about the South Side of Chicago except what they have seen or heard in the media. What Christians tend to do when they are working toward transformation is to attempt to theologize or only discuss complex issues. They never really step into the realities of how these issues are affecting real people. Mission Year gives young people an opportunity to live in neglected neighborhoods and experience the impact of these issues that we often only want to philosophize or theologize about. Many team members have said they value the opportunity to have names, faces, and relationships to connect with the issues that they are passionate about. However, when they get in relationship and begin to see the fullness of the neighborhoods, they become less overwhelmed with the brokenness and needs. In turn they begin to see the real beauty in these neighborhoods that they may have not seen previously.

One of my favorite moments throughout the year is our Urban Solitude Retreat, which gives team members the opportunity to spend the day in downtown Chicago just being present and organically learning from the people they meet. They are encouraged to notice those they would typically just pass by and to look for Jesus in the people and places we typically would not. While this day is challenging, it is a reminder that we often want to know the heart of God without ever having an experience with God's people. Jesus tells us repeatedly in Scripture that the people he came for are the most marginalized and disenfranchised in society.

Two team members spent time in conversation with a man named Max while downtown on the retreat. Max was a law-school graduate who had fallen on hard times and found himself homeless. They sat in a coffee shop and talked with Max for hours. They remarked that the longer they talked the less uncomfortable it felt to engage. These girls came back sharing about the conversation they had and their initial fear around the impromptu encounter. They admitted that if they had not been made to seek out this relationship, they would have missed out on it. These are the moments we desire for Mission Year team members—times when the only way we can learn hard truths is to be with the people who can teach us. Mission Year does not allow us to detach our learning from our living and will not allow the excuse that we need to learn before we can come live. It is only in our living with one another that we truly learn from one another.

One thing I hold dear from this organization is its central guiding question, which encapsulates both partnership and presence in one simple sentence: In this moment, how can I best love God and love people? This is the question that should drive each of us daily. It is this question that drives me as a pastor and drives Canaan as a community church. It is a question that should lead every Christian down a daily path of self-reflection: What is my best course of action if I am concerned about loving God and the people around me to the best of my ability? The power of partnership begins with the recognition that the choices we make, both good and bad, and the relationships we cultivate or destroy all have implications for those around us. If a church decides to be insular and concerned only with its congregants, while it may have great impact on the members of the church, the surrounding community may see the church as self-serving and prideful.

I encourage anyone who desires to learn what it means to practice presence in neglected neighborhoods to check out Mission Year and find out what it means to live and learn from the voices society and the church have typically not allowed to be heard.

LISTENING THEN LOVING

The poem also suggests that you cannot say you love someone if you have not listened to them. One of the main issues I have with well-meaning Christians is our abuse of the word *love*. We are quick to tell people how much we love them without ever attempting to listen to their stories or understand their life situations. I do not mean to insinuate that it is impossible to show love without a deep, intimate relationship. People do this every day. First responders run into burning buildings, gunfire, natural disasters, and other dangerous circumstances to save perfect strangers. When a natural disaster happens, we often see the best in humanity as total strangers risk their lives to save one another. This is love.

However, these instances do not discredit the transformative power of a genuine, long-term, loving relationship. Similar to first responders, churches would like to do quick, one-time, relief events that take very little personal investment or connection. We love our back-to-school events, block parties, drive-by-evangelism crusades, and short-term feeding outreaches. But when this becomes our primary way of connecting to the community, our churches merely become disconnected social-service entities. Even worse, they become disconnected religious institutions prescribing only spiritual solutions for individuals with physical, mental, and spiritual needs. Partnership is necessary so that we can address the holistic needs of the local communities to whom we are supposed to be listening.

It is the responsibility of the local church to be a proponent for the voice of the local community. This means that while congregations may partner with elected officials, social service organizations, and other community entities, they must first of all be committed to listening to and representing the people they live among and love. This may cause a strain in partner relationships at times when those with power make decisions that affect the local community negatively. We must respect the individuals in office and not discredit them or any of the work we may have done in partnership with them. However, the church must come out in opposition of any law, ordinance, or misuse of power perpetuated against our local community. We are to listen to the voices of the most marginalized. This will sometimes create uncomfortable positions where local congregations find themselves alternating between the role of reconciler and resister, if they genuinely seek to listen to and love their neighbors.

In 2015, Brandon Smith, a freelance journalist, and William Calloway, a community activist who is also an outspoken Christian, worked arduously to have dash-cam video footage released of the shooting of Laquan Macdonald by police officer Jason Van Dyke. The video footage showed Van Dyke shooting Laquan in the back sixteen times while running away. The officer claimed he was under attack and felt threatened by the young man. As if this scene itself weren't horrific enough, even worse is that the footage was never released, the officer was never punished, and elected officials allegedly hid the information because it was an election year and they knew it would affect their chances for reelection.

In response, two protests were planned within days of one another. One was organized by the combined efforts of Christian leaders in the city whose primary focus was to block off the Magnificent Mile, a stretch of high-end shopping and tourist attractions in downtown Chicago, during Black Friday, the top shopping day of the year. However, just a few days earlier a protest was planned by the leaders of the Black Lives Matter movement of Chicago. Young people all over the South and West Sides of Chicago gathered together downtown for a march culminating at the first district police station at 18th and State Street.

One of my congregants wanted to attend this march. He told me he was tired of sitting idly by and watching black lives being snatched away without repercussion. Not wanting him to go alone and realizing there may not be a huge church presence, I decided it was important for me to go too. We joined the march about halfway through its downtown route and added our voices to the chants of "Hey, hey, ho, ho, these killer cops have gotta go." I saw the megaphone passed between the hands of young activists passionately leading us down State Street, one of the most prominent thoroughfares in our city, and preparing us for a showdown with police officers in full riot gear. Ironically, there were officers on our left and right sides keeping us safe from oncoming traffic and making sure the parade route was clear as we marched in disdain of the system of policing that they were sworn to uphold.

Once we reached the front of the station, emotions began to run high and those passionate chants from minutes earlier turned to angry yelling, finger pointing, profane idioms, and threats of violence against the police officers. Some of the protestors had even walked up to the metal barricades and begun threatening officers to their faces. They were being told to step back and it was easy to see that this could escalate into something violent very quickly. Without thinking, I jumped in front of one of the protestors who was right in the face of an officer, and as I stood in front of him, I urged him to continue to scream but to scream at me. He grabbed my shoulder and tried to push me out of the way, but I refused to move. As he continued to scream loudly with tears streaming down his cheeks, I turned to the officer and said, "We appreciate your

service, and I know this must be hard, but we are rightfully angry."
I turned back and urged the man to continue screaming. I reminded
him that what happened to Laquan was wrong and we should be
angry. I once again turned to the officer and reminded her that she
was not the problem. It was what the uniform and the badge she
was wearing represented that was upsetting, and I urged her please
not to take it personally. I am not sure how much help I was that
day, but thankfully there were no physical altercations, and the only
casualty that night was the large Christmas tree downtown, which
the angry mob went on to partially destroy.

I learned that night that this is the uncomfortable position of
the local church. To stand in the middle of conflict knowing the
worth and need for all parties in partnership and holding ourselves,
as well as all others involved, accountable for our actions toward
one another. The local church, because of our love for everyone,
must stand as a bridge between the powerful and the powerless,
between those with the loudest voices and those who feel voiceless.
However, we must recognize that when we set ourselves up as a
reconciling bridge, we are destined to be walked on by both sides.

This is when we must steward our relationship equity. We must
use the influence from our long-term relationships and the power
that carries to do the reconciling work of the kingdom. Many organizations, community leaders, elected officials and religious
organizations will have well-meaning and well-thought-out plans,
especially in neglected neighborhoods. But often the most important
step will be missed, which is asking the residents what they desire
in the first place. This is what I mean when I say that entire neighborhoods have been forsaken by the church. It is not that there is
a shortage of local congregations in existence or new ones being
planted. The problem is that most local churches are so quick to
assume we know what people need that we don't take time to listen
to them. I have heard it stated that the people with the problems

are the people with the solutions. We want to help others, but we don't realize that the best thing we can do is to help others help themselves. Before we can love, we need to take time to listen.

LEADING BY FOLLOWING

We as Christians have to be okay with following, although that is hard for some of us to hear. When we look at the grassroots movements in this country, while there are exceptions, typically it is not the church that's leading the charge. Many of us, either because of our apathy or our need to be in control of every aspect of the movement, have given ourselves such a bad name that at this point no one even wants to listen to us—especially not the young people now leading these movements. If we are going to be part of the transformation of our neglected neighborhoods, then we have to be people of presence and learn to be followers. In greater Englewood it is obvious there is far more traction and transformation happening through community organizations than through churches and religious organizations. So we have decided to come alongside them and ask how we can be supportive resources to them on this journey. We do not have to be the leaders at the forefront. While we know transformation won't happen without the church, we do not believe that all transformation will come through the church.

I am often in discussions with Pastor Wayne Gordon of Lawndale Christian Community Church (LCCC) on the West Side of Chicago. Our neighborhoods, North Lawndale and West Englewood, share many of the same characteristics, assets, and issues. They are both majority African American neighborhoods bordering majority Latino communities and have had significant population decreases resulting in an abundance of vacant land and abandoned homes. Both communities are full of hardworking, tight-knit neighbors who take care of one another in unimaginable ways. They are full of God-honoring, people-loving residents fighting valiantly to reclaim the full narrative of their place and fight the internalization of the labels placed on their communities. The main difference is that LCCC has been coming alongside residents to empower them to make change for forty years now. For this reason, I consider Pastor Gordon, affectionately known as "Coach," to be a mentor in Christian community development even though we differ on the church's position in the transformation in the community.

If you visit LCCC, you will see the dramatic results of forty years of transformation that have happened through the church's involvement, including a health center, fitness center, recovery home, legal center, development corporation, full-scale pizzeria, and much more. Every building constructed and transformational organization created is considered a ministry of the church. This model has worked for LCCC for forty years and was my introduction to Christian community development. It should be celebrated. What I realized over the years in Englewood is that because of historic distrust, rather than being the center of attention, the church needed only to be present and partnering.

So when individuals come visit Canaan Community Church and ask about our various ministries, more often than not I respond by telling them about a partnership we have in our community or city. We partner with the Kusanya Café, and although it is not a ministry of Canaan, Phil Sipka, who led the charge to open it, is a great friend of our congregation. Canaan served as the café's fiscal agent, and there were hours of sweat equity from Canaan members assisting in building out and cleaning up prior to the grand opening. This is why Canaan members, just like other residents, recognize Kusanya as our café! While church members do not hold any positions or make any decisions for it, we are also partners with the Resident Association of Greater Englewood. Anyone who makes the decision to officially become a member of Canaan Community Church knows they are automatically signed up as a member of the resident association as well. We also partner with other organizations like the Voices of West Englewood, led by Ms. Gloria Williams, who put on the very first West Englewood Gospel Music Festival. While Canaan was heavily involved in the planning and implementation of the event, we made sure the community knew that the residents of West Englewood sponsored it. Canaan also partnered with Marion Williams Institute to provide second-chance high-school diplomas for those eighteen and older. One of the students who graduated from the Marion Williams Institute was Ture Johnson, a former student of mine when I taught at Harvard Elementary. His mother, Latanya Johnson, has an organization called Latanya and the Youth of Englewood. One summer she had trouble securing space in order to run her programming. Canaan was planning to do a summer youth program as well and had secured food service but we didn't publicize well and had very few children. She needed space and food and we needed children so we partnered together. It has grown into a beautiful partnership and on the wall of her new space is a beautiful picture of her young people playing on the steps of Canaan. Latanya said it hangs prominently in their foyer as a reminder of the kindness of the church. When we support our neighbors and become involved in their initiatives, the community sees that the church is serious about making our neighborhood better. We combat the belief that we are only concerned with growing our membership through church-sponsored events.

There is no need to reinvent the wheel because there are already good people doing good work in the community. Rather than

 constructing ministry opportunities, we spend our time partnering with people in the community who are already doing good work. Even when they don't recognize it as God's work, we do. We can be

involved in activities and events around the community held by individuals and organizations, even if we do not fully agree with everything they stand for, because we still believe they are doing God's work. Local churches need to get over the notion that everyone has to adhere to a Christian worldview if they are going to be transformational in today's society. There are many areas in which our communities need transformation. The church, while an integral component, need not believe we have all the answers.

In 2016 at the CCDA conference in Los Angeles, Dr. Brenda Salter McNeil said, "The church needs to understand that this generation is no longer looking for the singular, charismatic leader. They are looking for people to join in as they take the lead themselves. In the era of social media no one has to wait for someone else to take the lead."[1] While I agree that these young leaders are looking for us to follow them, we should also be eagerly looking forward to their leadership. We may not always agree with their tactics or philosophies, but we need their voices to lead us closer to the prosperity of our communities.

For the exiles in Jeremiah's story, as well as the Israelites after being freed from slavery in Egypt, it is the next generation that leads them fully out of captivity. This is why Jeremiah urges the exiles to pray to the Lord on behalf of Babylon. Babylon must thrive for the next generation to thrive. Israel could not assume anything about Babylon but had to pray for its prosperity and seek its welfare. In the same way we must not believe that we already know what our neighborhoods need and desire. We must seek the prosperity of our neighbors and be present in our neighborhoods; then we will begin to see how to pray on their behalf. One of the most dangerous prayers we can pray is an uninformed one. Let's not spend our time praying for an inadequate revitalization in our communities that neither our neighbors nor God desire. My prayer is that we will truly live with and learn from those around us, that

REORIENT OUR VISION TO SEE LIKE GOD

THE CHURCH-FORSAKEN PERSPECTIVE

*For surely I know the plans I have for you,
says the LORD, plans for your welfare and not
for harm, to give you a future with hope.*

JEREMIAH 29:11

*Blight, like beauty, is in the eye of the beholder,
and it happened, more often than not, that the
part of the city the businessmen thought was
blighted was the part where black people lived.*

MINDY THOMPSON FULLILOVE, MD

*I don't mean to sound morbid But I hate when
folks believe they found gold when They move
to a place where its quiet at night Quiet don't
mean safe plus what makes comfortable right?*

PASTAH J

SEEING THE WORLD THE WAY GOD DOES

My family and I had the opportunity to have a young college student, Mrs. Kayla Sutton, stay with us during the summer of 2013. She had visited Canaan with her college ministry, and although her college, Samford University, was in Birmingham, Alabama, her family lived in the north suburbs of Chicago. She took a liking to Canaan, Englewood, and my family, so she made the decision to live and work on the South Side for a summer to learn more about urban ministry and the principles of Christian community development.

While she stayed with us, we learned that she came from a rather affluent background. Her parents, understandably, were not especially enthusiastic about her choice to live in our inner-city community with strangers. My wife and I offered to speak with her parents to hopefully calm some of their fears as well as introduce ourselves to them. We wanted them to at least have an idea of who we were and who would be responsible for their daughter. We invited them over to dinner at our home but, unfortunately, they were unable to come. The next day we had a long talk with Kayla, and she admitted that she did not believe her parents would ever feel comfortable coming down to our neighborhood, especially not in the evening for dinner. After the conversation I asked her if she would set up an opportunity for us to visit them for dinner. I wanted them to know we felt it was extremely important for this conversation to happen. As a father I would have wanted to meet the family my daughter was living with for the summer. She agreed and we set up a dinner appointment for a few weeks later.

After nearly an hour drive north of Chicago, we pulled into the long driveway of their beautiful house and parked in front of the four-car garage. Once inside we met Kayla's entire family, her parents and her siblings, and we all sat down for dinner. After about an hour of small talk—laughing and sharing about our families and our respective churches—we began the uncomfortable conversation about Kayla's decision to live and work on the South Side. Kayla's father, Jerry, admitted that Kayla had always been different than his other children. She was the only girl and seemed to always think and behave differently. So although he was not excited about her decision, he was not surprised. His wife, Lynne, agreed with his sentiment and opened up by saying that unfortunately all she knew about the South Side of Chicago was what she heard on the news. Due to the negative coverage, especially of neighborhoods like Englewood, she couldn't help but worry about her daughter's safety. All their concerns were valid and understandable. They could only see my community through the perspective that had been set up for them, and that was one of brokenness, pain, and violence.

I looked up from our beautifully prepared dinner and around their immaculately decorated home. Then I looked back at the worried mother of four and asked her a serious question: "Do you think I am a good father?" She looked puzzled and a little taken aback by the question, so I asked again. "Do you think I am a good father?"

This time she seemed stunned and responded by saying, "I am not sure I am qualified to answer that."

I quickly responded, "Exactly. You have not spent enough time with my family to make that judgment. It would not be a fair assessment if you made one based on this one encounter. However, communities like Englewood have to deal with this on a continual basis. Millions of people have made judgments about our community and the thousands of residents who live there without any attempt to get to know us."

I could have admitted that my family had also made similar uneducated judgments about them and their community because of their large homes, immaculate lawns, four-car garages, and cul-de-sac-lined subdivisions. As a black male driving through their community, I was extremely nervous about being perceived as a threat or getting pulled over by police for any reason. There was never any real threat, but the perceived fear was real enough to keep me tense the entire drive. It may have been this same kind of fear that kept her parents from coming to our home a few weeks earlier. Although for very different reasons, neither of us felt comfortable coming to the home of the other.

We continued our conversation and ultimately came to the understanding that crossing our geographic, social, economic, and racial dividing lines was the beginning of easing our concerns and erasing our misinformed judgments. After the conversation was over, I presented them with a mixed-media piece of artwork I had created named *Bifocals* (see the beginning of this chapter). It was a small double canvas representing the skyline of Chicago. One canvas held one half of the skyline, represented in black and white with only two-dimensional features. The other canvas held the other half of the skyline in full color with three-dimensional elements such as trees and bushes. While both canvases are beautiful in their own right, neither of them gives us the full picture of the city. I explained that to me this is what it means to see the world the way God does. We often decide that we only want to see through one particular lens, and whichever lens we choose determines how we react to certain people and places. However, we need to broaden our vision and widen our perspective if we are going to be present with one another the way God desires. Just as we need both canvases for this artistic piece to make sense and to see its full beauty, we also need a broader perspective of the people and places around us.

This interaction began an amazing relationship between our families. Whenever I visit them, *Bifocals* is displayed prominently on their mantle, and we share a laugh about the initial awkwardness of our first meeting. Lynne and I are so glad that both of us stepped outside our comfort zones long enough to expose each other's biases. Jerry has come to visit Canaan and has participated in our Angels of Hope ministry where we visit with families of the incarcerated to provide support, prayer, and other resources. We have shared countless family celebrations together: birthdays, graduations, proms, anniversaries, and even engagements—which, of course, led to one of my proudest moments, when I was asked to preside over Kayla's wedding to her husband, Darion, and in turn become an even bigger part of their family structure. I will forever be thankful for Kayla's desire to reorient her vision and no longer see the South Side of Chicago or any other neglected neighborhood through a singular lens. She is an example of what can happen when we recognize that our view of the world is incomplete and needs to constantly be adjusted.

GOD'S GLORY AND HUMANITY'S BROKENNESS

In Jeremiah 29:11, God is reminding Israel that his ways are not their ways and his plans are not their plans. While they think they know what is best for themselves, where they should live, and where they should go, God wants them to see things from a broader perspective. We have to remember that God has a long-term view and doesn't see things the way we see them. The only way we can begin to see from this perspective is to believe that there is no place, person, or practice that God is unable to turn around for his glory. We often find ourselves, based on our own personalities and desires, categorizing certain people and places. If they remind us of something we value or have been told to value by societal standards, we connect their attributes to the glory of God—what I like to call "putting on our glory-of-God glasses."

As a young person this played out in how I saw living in the suburbs versus living in the inner city. In just about every television show, movie, or book, the wide expanse of suburban sprawl was lifted up as the better way to live. Whenever I would visit friends or family who lived outside the city, I would see how everything was seemingly beautiful and quiet. The grass was all the same height and everyone had big houses with beautiful valances in the windows and two-car garages. It seemed like every one of them was the perfect American family. They fit the usual statistics perfectly: two-parent household with two-and-a-half kids and a dog. I would stop and listen carefully and it would always be so quiet. I would think to myself that this must be what the glory of God looks like.

However, I was unable to see the same glory in my inner-city community. I would miss all the ways we were resiliently thriving despite the struggles we faced. I missed all the amazing community relationships created and the many ways I had been prepared to deal with the hardships of life because I had a mother who kept going no matter what life seemed to throw at us. I couldn't see the beautiful parks, artistic murals, community organizations, churches, and other religious institutions that were displaying the glory of God in my community. I only had on my glory-of-God glasses when I was in the suburbs, and I consistently took them off as soon as I was back in my own community. Of course, I conveniently had a separate pair of glasses to wear whenever I returned home.

We often take the Jeremiah 29:11 passage out of its exilic context to use for graduations, weddings, and other joyful life moments. We want to remind one another that God wants what's best for us and that we should look forward to prosperity. However, in context this verse is a reminder that God has a plan for us even in difficult circumstances, when things are not going the way we desired. If we want to reorient our perspective to see the way God sees we have to be able to trust the plan of God even when the brokenness of humanity is weighing on us heavily and things are not the way we had hoped.

This plays out in how I reacted to my own inner-city community mostly because of the lenses I saw through whenever I was there. Society's narrative had instructed me to wear my brokenness-of-humanity glasses in my neighborhood in stark contrast with my glorious perspective of suburban living. I would see trash on the ground and be frustrated that we were unable to pick up our own trash. I would see abandoned houses and vacant lots and understood why people did not want to live in my community. Although I personally never experienced any violence in high school, the narrative was that I was not safe. So I had to walk through a metal detector every day. I was worried about gang violence and crime as a young man so I learned what gang territories I would cross on my way to school. This was the dominant narrative that was perpetuated and so it was the narrative I believed. I did not have the understanding that while some of these experiences were real, they were also magnified because my chosen way of viewing my community was through the lens of brokenness.

Conversely, I was unable to see the brokenness in the suburbs when I would visit out there. It seems they were good at hiding their brokenness. It was masked well with manicured lawns and hidden behind those beautiful, valanced windows. There were issues with drugs, gangs, domestic violence, and crime in those communities as well. Lots of young people had run-ins with law enforcement; however, the difference was they were not treated as criminals before being convicted of a crime. I learned that the quietness of the neighborhood did not mean that the streets were safe or that they were not crying out for justice. Actually, the silence was deafening because no one was taking up the cause of the marginalized and oppressed in those communities. It was more important to maintain their reputation as a place of glory than to deal with the brokenness in their midst.

PUTTING ON OUR BIFOCALS

The issue with my perspective wasn't an inability to see the glory of God or the brokenness of humanity for I could clearly see both. The problem was that I chose my lens based on the situation. I realized what I needed to do, and this is the request I have been making of people all over the world the last few years: Take both pairs of lenses, crack them in half, and pull a Benjamin Franklin by putting the lenses together and making bifocals. If we want to see the world the way God does, then we have to realize that every person and every place displays both the glory of God and the brokenness of humanity at all times. If we are unable to see either, there is something wrong with our vision, not with the place or the person. When we can see the glory of God in a person or place, then we know what to thank God for. When we see the brokenness in a person or place, then we know what to ask God for. Whenever we enter a place or meet a new person, we must check to see if we have put on our bifocals.

Not only do bifocals help us to see multiple perspectives, but they also work to change the distance from which we see. Bifocal glasses can magnify things that are far away so that we can see clearer. This brings us back to the conversation of proximity and presence. When we characterize people and places from a distance, we can often only see one side of the narrative. We make up our minds about how we will categorize them solely based on what we have heard or have been told because we do not have any personal experience with the person or the place. But when we get closer to a person or a place we are able to see and experience them for ourselves and our characterizations become more complete and honest. God wants us to change our perspective of those around us—as if we were putting on bifocals—so that we can see clearer who they are and how they reflect both the glory of God and the brokenness of humanity. Each of us is a perfect example. While I am sure you are an amazing person and many times a day you reflect the glory of God in your actions and thoughts, if we were to spend any significant amount of time together, no matter how much we tried to impress one another, I am sure our brokenness would show up in some capacity.

God reminds us in Jeremiah 29:11 that there is an ultimate plan for us no matter where we are or whom we find ourselves with. No matter how difficult or strange those plans seem to us, they always include a future with hope. This is not to dismiss the freedom we have in Christ or our ability to make good or bad choices that affect where we find ourselves in life. In the words of Dr. King from his "Shattered Dreams" sermon, "Freedom is always within the framework of destiny. But there is freedom. We are both free and destined. Freedom is the act of deliberating, deciding, and responding within our destined nature."[1] It should not matter where God sends us or to whom. If we are going to see the world the way God does, then we will have to believe that the plan is to give us a future with hope and never to harm us. This type of faith and hope requires that we put on our bifocals daily. We must search for the way God is glorified by our present situation and the ways the brokenness of humanity is showing up. We are called to believe that even in our exilic situations God wants what's best for us. Paul echoes these sentiments in his letter to the church in Rome. Despite the persecution they were facing, he claims that "all things work together for good for those who love God, who are called according to his purpose" (Romans 8:28).

FAITHFULNESS AND HOPEFULNESS

I don't want to paint the picture that I don't ever struggle. I find myself wondering how God can be glorified by some of the things I see and endure in my community. With all the amazing things that have occurred in the greater Englewood community over the last ten years, I often still feel overwhelmed with the magnitude of need in our community. The need is often amplified by the political climate of the city, state, and country, as well as the global issues that impact us all. There have been many times when I have felt burned out by ministry and have been looking for any reason to hold on to my belief. In these times, I find myself holding on to God's desire for faithfulness. I engage in the work of loving my neighbors out of obligation and service, not necessarily because I believe anything is going to change.

I had the opportunity to visit the Equal Justice Initiative in Montgomery, Alabama, an organization "committed to ending mass incarceration and excessive punishment in the United States, to challenging racial and economic injustice, and to protecting basic human rights for the most vulnerable people in American society."[2] There I heard executive director Bryan Stevenson warn against solely working out of faithfulness. He said it could be damaging because those times often come at the expense of hope. He defined faithfulness as doing what you know to do because it is the right thing to do. Hopefulness is doing what you know to do because you expect transformation. Faithfulness allows you to continue to work even if it feels mundane and unfulfilling. Admittedly, there are times when this is necessary. We won't always feel encouraged or enthusiastic about where we are, whom we are with, or what we are called to do. However, we should always be trying to move toward hope, for hope breeds creativity. When we are working in the mindset of hope, we are more likely to think outside the box, try something new, or be energized by the opportunities ahead rather than frustrated by our present difficulties.

My close friend Angie Hong, multicultural worship leader and advocate for justice, says it this way in her blog entry titled "Bearings": "With hope, we can walk more fully into the reality of the Kingdom, where Jesus sits on the throne and everything is as it should be. With hope, we can live and flourish in the time of the 'now' but 'not yet.' With hope, it is possible to happily plant gardens and build houses even when we're in exile. But without hope, dreams and creativity wither away and die."[3]

NEW QUESTIONS

So yes, God commands us in Jeremiah 29:7 to seek the welfare of the city and pray to the Lord on its behalf, for in its welfare we will find our welfare. This is great—all of us would agree with this verse! This verse is not the problem for most of us, for it answers the ever-popular question of *what*. Our issue is with Jeremiah 29:4-6, which answers the terrifying questions of *where* and *with whom*. My fellow exiles, God commands us to love all the people and places in the world, not from a distance but from within!

This leads me to challenge us to ask different questions and seek answers in new ways. Will you stop only asking God *what* he wants you to do and begin asking *where* God might want you to do it and *with whom*? Will you stop only asking *what* you can do to change the world and start asking *where* and *with whom* in the world you might be changed the most? Will you stop asking *what* will make the biggest impact and start asking *where* and *with whom* could the biggest impact be made on you? Will you stop asking *what* is the most comfortable fit for you and start asking *where* you can go to be with those who make you the most uncomfortable? For nowhere in Scripture has God ever called us to be comfortable!

Many who are reading this have been on the journey toward practicing presence for quite a while. Like me, you may need encouragement to hang on for the long haul. In Jeremiah 29:10, God makes it clear that Israel's time in exile is not a short one. He says they will be in exile for seventy years before they are able to return to Jerusalem. Notice that there is no other promise made about Babylon other than that Israel's prosperity is tied up in Babylon's prosperity. There is no promise that a miraculous transformation will happen in Babylon, just that God is with them during their time of exile. However, we know that when people or places encounter God there is always transformation. I think the question being proposed here is: Can you be faithful even when the only thing changing is you?

So, my fellow exiles, it does not matter whether you are practicing presence in a diverse inner-city neighborhood or a sprawling suburban community, whether your place is in a rugged rural township or hipster-laden, urban landscape. It does not even matter if you are living and serving locally or trotting the globe graciously, or whether your primary concerns are foreign or domestic. For all of us who are practicing presence in neglected neighborhoods there are some basic principles we must keep at the center of our mission.

Remember that God is not concerned with success but faithfulness built on a foundation of hope. God never promised us success but has only asked us to be faithful and to remain hopeful. We must continue to honor God's process, plan, places, people, purpose, and perspective. The church has forsaken these directives long enough, looking instead for comfort and safety. When we seek to practice presence in neglected neighborhoods, we are living as countercultural witnesses to the power of the gospel.

Keep honoring God's original process of transformation, which hinges on us being present with one another. Jeremiah is clear that the first step in seeking the peace and welfare of the place you have been called is to build houses and live in them (Jeremiah 29:5). We are not called to seek community flourishing from a distance, going in and out of communities, unable to understand the residents' experience, but instead follow the process of Jesus and his incarnational ministry: "The Word became flesh and blood, and moved into the neighborhood" (John 1:14 *The Message*). Jesus left the comfort of the throne of God to enter into the messiness and frustration of humanity. He knew that transformation would begin by understanding what humanity had to endure as well as what humanity had to offer. The creation of a group of followers that turned the world upside down began with the single decision to be totally present with them regardless of what it cost.

Continue to honor God's original plan, which is to care about the whole person and not just their soul. Jeremiah urges Israel to plant gardens and eat what they produce (Jeremiah 29:5). God was just as concerned about their physical well-being as their spiritual well-being. Pastors Charles and Florence Mugishe could only understand why saving souls wasn't enough when they began to practice presence in Rwanda. They saw that people accepting Jesus as their Savior while still having no home, no food, and no way out of their situation was not good enough news. The creation of Africa New Life Ministries only happened when the directive to be concerned about the health of the whole person became clear. The growth and health of the church is contingent on the growth and health of the people. As Jesus performed miracles like healing the sick, giving sight to the blind, making the lame walk, and raising the dead, his concern for their physical well-being became intricately connected to his care for their spiritual well-being. We must continue to love people holistically. This is the road to true transformation and is good news for everyone who experiences it.

Continue to honor all of God's places, especially the neglected neighborhoods all over the world. Jeremiah urges Israel to marry and have children, then to allow those children to marry, so that they may increase in number there and not decrease. I have watched the impact a generational investment in a community can make. The transformation is not just in the community but in the fabric of the family. As your family becomes identified with your place, your concern for that place begins to grow. In his book *Real Hope in Chicago*, Pastor Wayne "Coach" Gordon begins and ends with the same sentence: "I love living in Lawndale."[4] Forty years later it is amazing to see how true that statement is for him and his family. I recently visited Lawndale Christian Community Church for their fortieth anniversary celebration and was so impressed by the Gordon family. Coach and his wife Anne sat proudly in their front-row seats with their children and grandchildren gathered behind them. Their love for their church and their community was evident, and you could tell that they were proud to be identified with North Lawndale. I also looked around and saw the number of families that have grown in Lawndale from the church's investment in that place. All around the church and community there are families that have been formed and saved due to the work of ministries like the Hope House. Because there was a Christ-centered recovery home right in the neighborhood, there are many fathers who have been reunited with their families after overcoming the effects of drug abuse. Wives reconnected to husbands. Children reconnected to fathers. Families made whole. This is what it looks like for the church to increase and not decrease our presence in a place.

Continue to love all God's people, establishing genuine relationships and challenging any uninformed or monolithic stereotypes. Jeremiah urges Israel to seek the peace and welfare of the city where they have been sent into exile. This means they must learn to value Babylonian social structures, backgrounds, languages, identities, customs, and political climate. While people may be different, it does not mean that they are any less valuable to the kingdom of God. Willie and Geraldine have taught our congregation so much about unconditional love and valuing everyone's contributions to our church community. Their presence in our church has helped us to understand how to honor people's gifts while walking with them through their struggles. We have watched their love for God grow and our patience with people grow. There is mutual transformation happening as we seek one another's welfare. This is also why churches should partner with residents, community organizations, law enforcement, and government officials. These partnerships are for the collective flourishing of our community. Transformation happens when the entire community works together and values every person's contribution.

Continue in the original purpose of the church, which is to be transformative representatives in our communities and the world by loving God with everything and loving our neighbors as we love ourselves. Jeremiah closes out this part of the letter reminding Israel to pray on behalf of Babylon, for in its welfare they will find their welfare (Jeremiah 29:7). We must fight arduously against the urge to create a false dichotomy between the church and surrounding community. We must be so interwoven into the fabric of the neighborhood that it is obvious our futures are inextricably tied together. My family has benefited immensely from the transformations in Englewood and has worked equally as hard to see them come to pass.

We have built a house and are living in it, but we are also praying for every one of our neighbors to have a nice house on a loving block. We have helped to plant gardens, start co-ops, open cafés and grocery stores. We are still praying that every resident has access to affordable, healthy food options within a reasonable distance. We partner with a myriad of organizations to provide services and opportunities for youth and young adults. And we are still praying that any young person in need of mentorship, educational enrichment, restorative justice opportunities, or just a listening ear will have a place to turn. We have worked hard to change the narrative being told about our community. We also pray that more Englewood residents will see their faces on billboards and become champions for broadcasting the #goodinenglewood and a contributing part of #englewoodrising. We are praying to the Lord for Englewood because we know as it continues to prosper we too will prosper.

Lastly, continue to see the world from God's perspective, which is the ability to see the fullness of humanity and reflection of divinity in every person and place. Every morning before our feet hit the floor, we must each put on our bifocals so that we are able to see the glory of God and brokenness of humanity in every situation. When we see in this way, we are freed to dream even when things around us are not perfect. I remember walking through an abandoned firehouse more than ten years ago with Pastor Phil Jackson of The House Covenant Church. At that time "Tha House" was the only hip-hop worship experience in Chicago. As Phil and I walked through this firehouse, he dreamed of it becoming a fully functional community arts center with classes in visual arts, dance, music, and culinary arts. He walked through what used to be the kitchen and said, "Don't you see it, Jay? Young men from off the streets who used to be shooters now being chefs. Young African American men in white chef coats and hats preparing delicious food for their own community." I didn't see it. This was during the time when Chicago was being branded with the title of Chi-raq, and many of the young men in our communities were embracing and embodying it. Phil knew that the young men he was working with had some serious issues and were in need of the love of Jesus to work through them. However, he also knew they were created in the image of God and had greatness within them if only they had the opportunity to show it.

The Firehouse Community Arts Center opened about five years after this initial conversation, but it was just recently when Phil saw his biggest dream come to pass. In partnership with Sweet Baby Ray's barbecue sauce, the Firehouse culinary arts program began in a new, state-of-the-art kitchen. Phil walked me through the building again and there they were—young men who used to be shooters had become chefs. I was looking at young African American men in white chef coats and hats preparing delicious food for their own community. Jeremiah 29:11 came alive on this day: "For surely I know the plans I have for you, says the LORD, plans for your welfare and not for harm, to give you a future with hope." We invest in neglected neighborhoods even when we know all is not well because we believe that God has plans for us, plans for our welfare and not our harm. When we, like Pastor Phil, are honest about the beauty and brokenness in our communities, it frees us up to dream. Regardless of the circumstances, we can pursue the best for our neighbors because we know that God has a plan and that gives us hope.

My desire for each of us is that we would wake up every day and put on our bifocals, for that is the only way to overcome our natural bias even as Jesus followers. We must recognize that God's plans for Israel's welfare were equally as true in exile as they were in Jerusalem. This truth is the elixir that can quell our insatiable thirst for comfort. God does not need us to be in comfort in order for us to prosper. As a matter of fact, God prefers the opposite, so that when prosperity comes, we are unable to take the credit. We have been called to be present in the places that most people do not want to go because we know our welfare is not tied up in our comfort but in our love for God and each other. For that reason, wherever we are, we bring with us the hope of Christ.

There are no God-forsaken places. And when God's people practice presence in the neglected neighborhoods all around us, we can say with confidence that there are no church-forsaken places either.

Church Forsaken by Jade Brooks

ACKNOWLEDGMENTS

To all of my friends who pushed me to write this book, I am indebted to you for believing in me and the power of my story. There are so many of you that I don't want to begin to name you all, but you know who you are and know that I am so thankful for who you are.

To my entire IVP team, you all are amazing! I am so thankful for this journey, and I am still trying to convince myself this is real. Thank you for amplifying the voices of people of color and believing our stories and insights need to be heard.

To the greater Englewood community, I am so proud of the amazing collective work we have done. I pray that I have honored the ways you have taught me what it means to truly seek the welfare of our community.

To Rev. Dr. Lacy Simpson Jr., thank you for seeing something in me that I couldn't even see in myself. I am thankful for you.

To Canaan Community Church, thank you for accepting and loving me just as I am. May we continue to love God, love people, and make disciples together while being the church where love makes the difference.

To my extended family, thank you so much for always being there for me and supporting me as God has continued to shape me.

To my siblings, we truly are a modern family! Each of you is special and has played a unique part in who I am.

To my mom, thanks for sacrificing and providing the rare opportunities that led to who I am today and for showing me what unconditional love looks like. To my dad, thanks for persevering and showing that fatherhood does not take perfection, just the effort to be present.

To my daughters, Jasmine and Jade, I love you more than life itself. Thank you for sharing your dad with so many people. Your sacrifice has led to this amazing reminder that with God anything is possible.

To my beautiful wife, Michéal, thank you for going on this unbelievable journey with me. I couldn't ask for a better partner. We have been through so much together, and you have never left my side. From architect, to teacher, to pastor and now writer and speaker, no matter where life takes me, you truly are my ride or die! I love you so much, and I promise that as long as there is breath in my body, I will be by your side.

NOTES

FOREWORD

[1]Glenn Clark, *The Man Who Talks with the Flowers: The Intimate Life Story of Dr. George Washington Carver* (Start Publishing, 2013). Kindle ed.

INTRODUCTION: FROM THE MIND OF AN EXILE

[1]Mark T. Mulder, *Shades of White Flight: Evangelical Congregations and Urban Departure* (New Jersey: Rutgers Press, 1979), 77.

[2]"Things Done Changed," track 2 on The Notorious B.I.G, *Ready to Die* (Bad Boy Records, 1994).

[3]James O. Stampley, *Challenges with Changes: A Documentary of Englewood* (Chicago: n.p., 1979).

[4]OMF International US, Twitter post, April 15, 2012, 6:00 a.m., https://twitter .com/omfus/status/191511422394576896.

I WELCOME HOME

[1]Sheila A. Bedi, "Lawlessness—of Chicago Police—Helps Keep Cycle of Incarceration Alive," *Crain's Chicago Business*, July 20, 2015, www.chicago business.com/article/20150720/OPINION/150719886/lawlessness -of-chicago-police-helps-keep-cycle-of-incarceration-alive.

[2]J. Sunshine and T. R. Tyler, "The Role of Procedural Justice and Legitimacy in Shaping Public Support for Policing," *Law & Society Review* 37 (2003): 513-48.

[3]Robert J. Sampson and Charles Loeffler, "Punishment's Place: The Local Concentration of Mass Incarceration," *Daedalus* 139, no. 3 (2010): 20-31.

[4]Dominique Gilliard, *Rethinking Incarceration: Advocating for Justice That Restores* (Downers Grove, IL: InterVarsity Press, 2018), 26.

2 THAT'S NOT MY DREAM

[1]Paul Jargowsky, "Architecture of Segregation: Civil Unrest, the Concentration of Poverty, and Public Policy," The Century Foundation, August 7, 2015, http://apps.tcf.org/architecture-of-segregation/.

[2]Anne Lamott, *Bird by Bird: Some Instructions on Writing and Life* (New York: Anchor Books, 1995), 22.

3 CO-OPS, CAFÉS, GARDENS, AND GROCERY STORES

[1]Natalie Y. Moore, *The South Side: A Portrait of Chicago and American Segregation* (New York: St. Martin's Press, 2016), 149.

[2]Moore, *South Side*, 143.

4 WHY SAVING SOULS AIN'T ENOUGH

[1]"Landmark Designation Report: Ebenezer Missionary Baptist Church," Commission on Chicago Landmarks, June 2, 2011, www.cityofchicago .org/content/dam/city/depts/zlup/Historic_Preservation/Publications /Ebenezer_Missionary_Baptist_Church.pdf.

[2]Albert E., Brumley, "I'll Fly Away," (1929), 2014, www.popularhymns.com /ill_fly_away.php.

[3]John M. Perkins, *Beyond Charity: The Call to Christian Community Development* (Grand Rapids: Baker Books, 1993), 18.

[4]This paragraph originally appeared in a section I coauthored in Bethany Harris, *Overview of the Philosophy of Christian Community Development* (Chicago: Christian Community Development Association, 2011).

[5]Glen Stassen, D. M. Yeager, and John Howard Yoder, *Authentic Transformation: A New Vision of Christ and Culture* (Nashville: Abingdon Press, 1996), 74.

[6]Paul Tillich, *Theology of Culture* (New York: Oxford University Press, 1959), 201.

[7]Bryant Meyers, *Walking with the Poor: Principles and Practices of Transformational Development* (Maryknoll, NY: Orbis, 2011), 85.

[8]Harris, *Overview of the Philosophy of Christian Community Development*, 27-28.

[9]Howard Thurman, *Jesus and the Disinherited* (Nashville: Abingdon, 1949), 12.

[10]Thurman, *Jesus and the Disinherited*, 13.

[11]Thurman, *Jesus and the Disinherited*, 108.

5 GOD, HAVE YOU LOOKED OUT YOUR WINDOW?

[1]Martin Luther King Jr., *Strength to Love* (Minneapolis: Fortress, 2010), 138.

6 PROMISING PLACE

[1]Steven P. Lancaster and James M. Monson, *Regional Study Guide: Introductory Map Studies in the Land of the Bible* (Rockford, IL: Biblical Backgrounds, Inc., 2014), 17, www.juc.edu/pdf/study_guide.pdf.

[2]As defined by the Seoul Declaration on Diaspora Missiology.

[3]Chimamanda Ngozi Adichie, "The Danger of a Single Story," TED Global, July 2009, www.ted.com/talks/chimamanda_adichie_the_danger_of_a_single_story.

[4]See "Failing Grade," Oprah.com, April 11, 2006, www.oprah.com/world/failing-grade/all.

7 NO MORE OUTREACH

[1]"Jesus Walks," Kanye West (Sony Music, 2004).

[2]Hezekiah Walker, "I Need You to Survive," *Family Affair 2: Live at Radio City Music Hall* (New York: Verity Records, 2002).

[3]"Peter Pan," track 2 on Sho Baraka, *Talented 10th* (Lions and Liars Music, 2013).

[4]*Feel Rich: Health is the New Wealth,* directed by Peter Spirer (Feel Rich Films, 2017).

8 AIN'T A THAT GOOD NEWS?

[1]See the *Encyclopedia Britannica* article "Five Percent Nation," www.britannica.com/topic/Five-Percent-Nation.

[2]"Family Feud," track 6 on *4:44* (Roc Nation, 2016).

[3]Martin Luther King Jr., *Strength to Love* (Minneapolis: Fortress, 2010), 35.

9 SHUT DOWN THE CHURCHES

[1]R.A.G.E. Englewood (@join_RAGE), "The churches need to step up in Englewood and @PastahJ is the exception and should be the rule . . . #RealTalkWithRAGE," Twitter, June 16, 2016, https://twitter.com/Join _RAGE/status/743606874868588544.

[2]Jonathan Brooks (@pastahj), "Although the #inconvenienttruth behind this post is not missed on me," Instagram, June 17, 2016, www.instagram .com/p/BGxJttsrzjD/?tagged=ssslove.

[3]"Welcome to Englewood Rising," www.englewoodrising.com (accessed April 30, 2018).

10 THE POWER OF PARTNERSHIP

[1]Brenda Salter McNeil, 2016 Christian Community Development Association conference, Los Angeles, https://ccda.org/product/brenda.

[2]Dwight D. Eisenhower, "Remarks at the Annual Conference of the Society for Personnel Administration," May 12, 1954, www.presidency.ucsb.edu /ws/index.php?pid=9884&st=&st1=.

CONCLUSION: SEEING THE WORLD THE WAY GOD DOES

[1]Martin Luther King Jr., *Strength to Love* (Minneapolis: Fortress, 2010), 91.

[2]Equal Justice Initiative, "About EJI," www.eji.org/about-eji (accessed April 30, 2018).

[3]Angie Kay Hong, "Bearings," *Angie Hong* (blog), January 12, 2017, www .angiekayhong.com/2017/01/12/bearings/.

[4]Wayne L. Gordon, *Real Hope in Chicago* (Grand Rapids: Zondervan, 1995), 15.

ABOUT THE AUTHOR

 **Jonathan Brooks ("Pastah J")** is senior pastor of Canaan Community Church in Chicago's Englewood neighborhood. He has a master of divinity in Christian community development from Northern Seminary, was an art and architecture teacher with Chicago Public Schools, and is a recording artist with the hip-hop group Out-World. He and his family live in West Englewood.

Contact Jonathan at:
www.pastahj.com
@pastahj on Instagram, Twitter, and Facebook
www.canaancommunitychurch.org

C|C CHRISTIAN COMMUNITY
D|A DEVELOPMENT ASSOCIATION

The Christian Community Development Association (CCDA) is a network of Christians committed to engaging with people and communities in the process of transformation. For over twenty-five years, CCDA has aimed to inspire, train, and connect Christians who seek to bear witness to the Kingdom of God by reclaiming and restoring underresourced communities. CCDA walks alongside local practitioners and partners as they live out Christian Community Development (CCD) by loving their neighbors.

CCDA was founded in 1989 under the leadership of Dr. John Perkins and several other key leaders who are engaged in the work of Christian Community Development still today. Since then, practitioners and partners engaged in the work of the Kingdom have taken ownership of the movement. Our diverse membership and the breadth of the CCDA family are integral to realizing the vision of restored communities.

The CCDA National Conference was birthed as an annual opportunity for practitioners and partners engaged in CCD to gather, sharing best practices and seeking encouragement, inspiration, and connection to other like-minded Christ-followers, committed to ministry in difficult places. For four days, the CCDA family, coming from across the country and around the world, is reunited around a common vision and heart.

Additionally, the CCDA Institute serves as the educational and training arm of the association, offering workshops and trainings in the philosophy of CCD. We have created a space for diverse groups of leaders to be steeped in the heart of CCD and forge lifelong friendships over the course of two years through CCDA's Leadership Cohort.

CCDA has a long-standing commitment to the confrontation of injustice. Our advocacy and organizing is rooted in Jesus' compassion and commitment to Kingdom justice. While we recognize there are many injustices to be fought, as an association we are strategically working on issues of immigration, mass incarceration, and education reform.

To learn more, visit www.ccda.org/ivp

Titles from CCDA

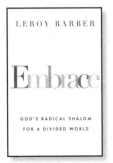

Embrace
978-0-8308-4471-5

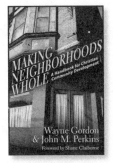

*Making
Neighborhoods Whole*
978-0-8308-3756-4

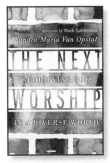

The Next Worship
978-0-8308-4129-5

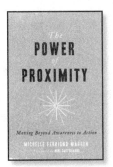

*The Power of
Proximity*
978-0-8308-4390-9

*Rethinking
Incarceration*
978-0-8308-4529-3

*Seeing Jesus in
East Harlem*
978-0-8308-4149-3

*Welcoming Justice
(expanded edition)*
978-0-8308-3479-2

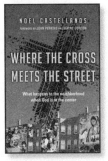

*Where the Cross
Meets the Street*
978-0-8308-3691-8

White Awake
978-0-8308-4393-0

VOICES

PROJECT

The Voices Project gathers leaders of color who influence culture (the church, education, art, entertainment, politics, and business) for important conversations about the current challenges and triumphs within communities of color and our role as cultural influencers. We train and promote leaders of color to offer voice to culture and society.

TRAINING AND PROMOTING

We provide insight, on how to be effective in leadership within one's respective area of cultural influence in a way that is rooted in history and experience of people of color. Additionally we connect leaders of color to leadership opportunities that are based in their areas of expertise within a domain of cultural influence.

INITIATIVES

- Mentorship or small group training with Voices staff (ongoing)
- Publishing company (ongoing)
- Bi-annual leadership gathering (January and August)
- Voices Conference (May)
- Northwestern college tour (October)
- Monthly newsletter (ongoing)

THE VOICES PROJECT
255 SW Bluff Dr
Bend, OR 97702
http://www.voices-project.org/

 https://twitter.com/jointhevoices

 https://www.facebook.com/JoinTheVoices/

https://www.instagram.com/jointhevoices/

132959